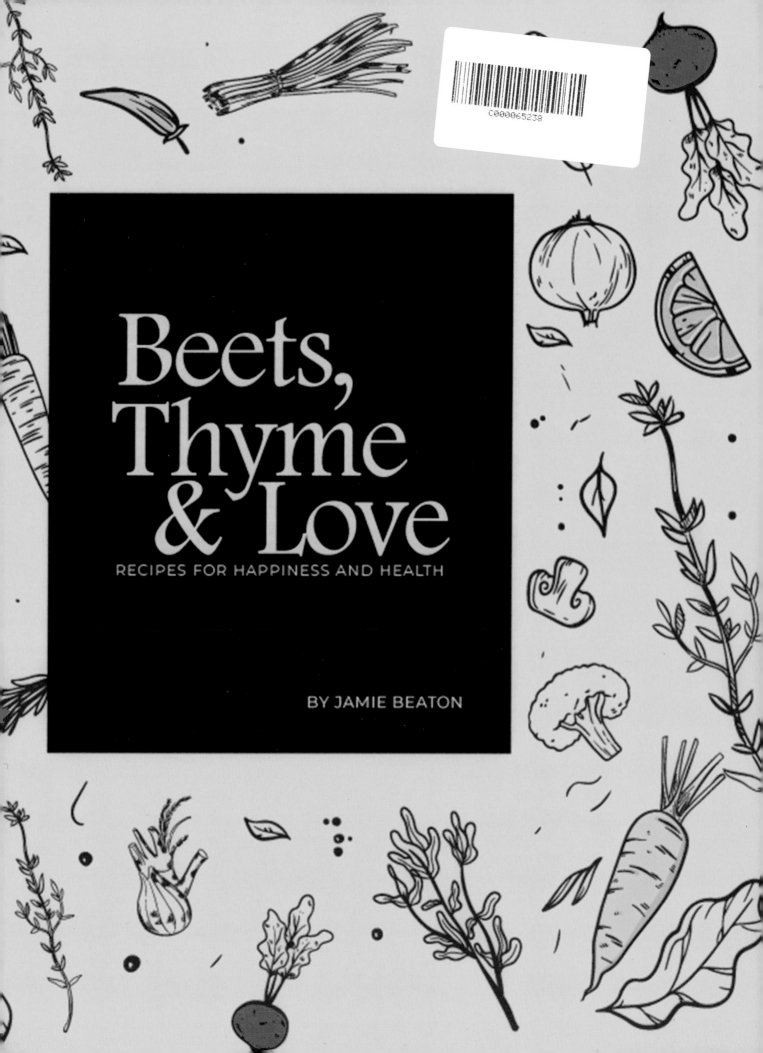

Beets, Thyme & Love

RECIPES FOR HAPPINESS AND HEALTH

BY JAMIE BEATON

Balboa Press books may be ordered through booksellers or by contacting:

Balboa Press
A Division of Hay House
1663 Liberty Drive
Bloomington, IN 47403
www.balboapress.co.uk
UK TFN: 0800 0148647 (Toll Free inside the UK)
UK Local: 02036 956325 (+44 20 3695 6325 from outside the UK)

Because of the dynamic nature of the Internet, any web addresses or links contained in this book may have changed since publication and may no longer be valid. The views expressed in this work are solely those of the author and do not necessarily reflect the views of the publisher, and the publisher hereby disclaims any responsibility for them.

ISBN: 978-1-9822-8371-1 (sc)
978-1-9822-8372-8 (e)

Print information available on the last page.

Balboa Press rev. date: 06/28/2021

BALBOA.PRESS
A DIVISION OF HAY HOUSE

Contents

Desserts and Sweet Snacks 101

Let food be your medicine and medicine your food.

—Chronnix

Foreword

Have you ever had one of those moments where you meet someone for the first time yet feel like you have known them your whole life? That's exactly how I felt when I first met Jamie at Vegfest London in 2019. In an exhibition hall full of selfie-takers and YouTube Hall of Famers, Jamie's presence cut through the bravado like a knife through vegan butter. He was modest, unassuming, yet radiating kindness and gratitude. His deep blue eyes held no secrets and felt like oceans of calm. His shoulders were broad and strong, yet his heart was wide open.

As we chatted like old friends, I was struck by Jamie's energy and zest for life. One could only assume that health and vitality were his birthright. Little did I know that it was not something that had always come easy to him.

It was only as our friendship deepened that I learnt more about Jamie's journey from an overweight and unhappy chef feeling lost in life to a healthy and vibrant being living with complete purpose and clarity. It was a long and winding road, littered with obstacles and challenges, and I have no doubt that Jamie will be the first to tell you he made his fair share of mistakes along the way. But in many ways, this is his superpower. Jamie is living proof that anyone can create abundance in their physical, mental, and spiritual lives, no matter where you are or how hard it may seem right now.

Beets, Thyme, and Love is a complete collection of the habits and methodologies (and of course, the food!) that turned Jamie's life around. Read them, absorb them, and practice them, and I'd bet my last piece of his famous French toast that they'll do the same for you too.

Josh Bolding
Cofounder of Vivo Life

Introduction

For most of my life, I ate meat and dairy multiple times a day. I enjoyed all the things most people do: steak, roasts, sausages, cream, cheese, and so on. I enjoyed it, and I didn't see why I shouldn't have it.

For most of my life, I have been overweight or obese. My diet certainly didn't help, but when I would be in phases of being active, I believed I needed animal-based protein to help me get stronger. As a foodie, and having previously worked as a chef, I also believed food wouldn't taste good without meat or dairy products. After all, the secret to French cooking is butter, butter, butter! How could food taste good without it, and would I want to live without it?

Most of us know that we should get five servings of fruit and vegetables a day, with new information coming out all the time saying it should be seven, eight, or ten. However, with the culture in Britain for meat and *two* veg, many of us aren't even hitting five a day.

I knew eating more vegetables and less meat would be better for my health, so I tried to have two or three meat-free days a week after a New Year's resolution. This was surprisingly easy for me and I enjoyed it, but I was still consuming a lot of dairy. I increased my vegetarian days to five a week, but my vegetable and fruit intake was probably only just over five a day.

I was in a phase where I was really interested in getting fit and "healthy" (which can mean so many different things to different people). When I came across an interview with a footballer for Manchester United who had turned vegan, I was shocked. I didn't believe you could be a high-performing professional athlete and be vegan. Where would the protein come from? In the interview, he said he was stronger, leaner, and recovered quicker because of his diet. Isn't that something everyone would like?

The article mentioned that my favourite footballer in the world, Lionel Messi, also ate a plant-based diet! I was even more shocked and googled it. Not only was Messi eating a plant-based diet, so were a whole load of high-performing athletes, from Lewis Hamilton and Novak Djokovic to American footballers and professional bodybuilders. Yet the question in my head remained the same: How could they reach that level of physical fitness with no meat?

And so my journey into a plant-based diet began. I read a number of books and articles, finding out that not only is protein abundant in plants, but plants combine protein with a whole host of other vitamins and nutrients that nourish the body. I struggled to find recipes that would meet my protein requirements for an active lifestyle or ingredients that were easily accessible. I tried recipes and tweaked them, learning more about ingredients and how to adapt them to create textures that I was familiar with, like cream or cheese sauce. It was almost like learning how to cook from scratch again, but this time every plate of food would help me become leaner, stronger, and healthier from the inside out.

I started creating my own recipes to meet my own cravings and needs. I felt great, and I wanted to share them. Everyone wants to eat tasty food, but if it can be healthy and nourishing too, what could be better? And so I present to you some of my favourite recipes to give you meals that should help you eat more plants in a healthy, tasty, easy, and fun way. Whether you are looking to move to one plant-based meal a week or more, my aim is to give you the belief and knowledge that a plant-based diet can be as tasty as the meat and dairy diet we have been accustomed to.

Planting the Way to Success

My journey to health didn't start with plants. To make long-lasting, sustainable changes, you need strong foundations that can handle the earthquakes that life throws at you. It starts with learning to love yourself. This may seem simple, but if you see yourself in *any* negative way, you are less likely to achieve the health and life that you want.

It is only now, in a healthy and happy place, that I truly see the lack of love I showed myself and my body. Overeating comfort food to create short-term happiness only led me to a more unhappy place. Once you start recognising these behaviours, you are halfway there. Having a bit more knowledge as to why we do this will hopefully help you even more.

Let's Talk About Stress, Baby!

Our bodies naturally crave salt, fat, and sugar. They have been doing this for thousands of years and won't stop anytime soon. But why? How can we use that to our advantage? Thousands of years ago, our hunter-gatherer ancestors needed salt, fat, and sugar to survive. Salt naturally exist in many plants as well as animals that ate the plants. Fats exist in nuts and seeds, and sugars in fruit and vegetables.

When our ancient ancestors would be at risk of harm, the fight-or-flight mode kicked in to protect their lives. After that stress response, they found the foods their bodies needed to survive. Then those fats and sugars could be stored in the body to keep them going and keep death and starvation away in case a life-at-risk situation happened again. It was a necessity to live!

The stressors our ancestors faced are extremely different from what we face on a day-to-day basis. Stress has taken a completely different form. So many people face stress multiple times a day, but the way our bodies process it is the same as they did thousands of years ago. The hormone cortisol is produced, and signals are sent to the brain to say that we need salt, fat, and sugar to get over this life-threatening stress (as well as some potentially aggressive behaviour to keep that bear away).

On top of that, cortisol tells the body that it can't risk losing the fat it already has. That fat may be needed in an emergency, especially if stress continues. The stress we face mostly isn't life-threatening, but we will go in search of salt, fat, and sugar nevertheless. These can probably be easily found in your fridge, or if not, at a nearby shop where we will find the crisps, chocolate, biscuits, and sugary drinks or alcohol (plenty of sugars and carbohydrates there!) to satisfy our needs.

So now that we know this, what can we do? Our bodies will always need salt, fat, and sugar; we just don't need it to come from crisps and chocolate. Lots of food contains all of it in different amounts. After I do a workout, my most basic recovery drink contains banana, peanut butter, and a pinch of salt. I drink this to replenish glycogen and electrolytes, but should I finish my workout in a stressed state, my body is getting what it needs.

Stress is everywhere in our lives: news, alerts on our phone, messages, arguments, work deadlines, bills, relationships, traffic jams. Even healthy exercise creates stress, but if we can't recover from it, we won't get stronger. We can't get away from stress, but there are ways we can handle it better. Here are my top tips:

1. **Breathe**

   We can all breathe, and it's free—but with focused, slower, deeper breaths, we engage the parasympathetic nervous system. Breathing in slowly for four seconds, holding for four, and exhaling for four seconds, holding for four seconds, and repeating (also known as box breathing) is one of the easiest ways to relax. Try it now for two minutes.

   How do you feel now? Hopefully, you weren't in a stressed state when you started reading this chapter, but even so, you should be more relaxed just from two minutes of box breathing. This is good for the brain as well as the body and can be practiced as many times as you want—while making a cup of coffee or tea, when at the photocopier, before making a phone call, in a traffic jam, before you eat, and my favourite time, before I sleep. It helps the mind and body relax and calm down. Give it a go and, most importantly, keep it up. Don't save it for the stressed times.

Another great option is the Wim Hof method. This method isn't just about breathing, it is also about cold exposure and commitment. The breathing method itself is incredibly easy: it involves taking thirty to forty deep breaths in before holding your breath for longer than you probably ever thought possible. The result is a chemical reaction that helps boost your mood, your immune system, and many other things. It has all been backed by science. I practice these methods daily. There is plenty of free information and an app at www.wimhofmethod.com.

2. **Be Grateful**

Every day, I write down a minimum of three things I am grateful for from that day. It doesn't have to be anything like winning the lottery. Hearing a song you like, seeing an animal, having the sunshine on your face, drinking a good cup of coffee, having a catch-up with a friend, watching a good film or TV show—these are all micro moments we enjoy every day, but unless we make an effort to stop and recall them, they are easily lost. I was amazed by the profound effect they have on my mental health, even when I thought it was in a good state anyway.

Give it a go now. What three things are you grateful for today? Do it again tomorrow and try to keep it up for the next thirty days, then look back. Like breathing, you don't need to save this for when you are stressed or sad. Doing it on a daily basis will help build resilience to make it harder for you to get stressed or sad.

3. Keep a Journal

Getting thoughts out of your head and onto paper can be a really beneficial and simple practice to create space in the mind and create calm and clarity. Journaling can be done in many ways, and I struggled to find a place to start. At the most simple, I do four things in the morning: I get out my coloured markers and go back to yesterday's journal page. I reflect on what I was grateful for that day and what was amazing or made the day amazing. Then I move on to the current day, where I write five things I want to get done today, then what I am grateful for and anything that was already amazing in my day. If I get a chance to, I will also write down an inspirational quote, often ones I've highlighted in books I have been reading.

4. Practice Meditation and Mindfulness

This was one of the biggest changes in my life. I never thought I would be someone who meditated. Even the first time I tried it, I thought my mind was too busy to be able to meditate, not understanding that was *why* I needed to meditate! Thankfully, I downloaded an app and committed to doing ten days.

After four to six days, my awareness was already much greater. I was noticing everything around me so much more, and I felt more able to be present in that moment and appreciate it. As with most things in life, I let my meditation practice slip a little, but I noticed it so much. From that moment, it has been rare that I miss a day.

As with most of these tips, daily practice builds resilience. You don't even need to do it for a long time. When I first started, I would do ten minutes during my lunch break. There are a number of apps with free trials or YouTube videos, so give it a go. The app I use (Headspace) has an option for three-minute mediations. Surely we all deserve to give ourselves at least three minutes a day. Try committing to it for ten days in a row and see if it works for you.

For those who are looking to lose weight and keep it off, some scientific studies have shown that practicing mindfulness can help people lose weight as well as reduce anxiety. I can certainly testify to that.

5. Do Yoga and Qigong

Most mornings, I start my day with yoga (often for not much more than ten minutes). I find it helps me start my day in a positive way by dedicating time to myself first thing in the morning. There can be a number of similarities between yoga and meditation, but I find the two complement each other well. Yoga stimulates the body in a gentle way and over time can help build strength and mobility, as well decrease stress. When I have done an intense workout, I finish with some yoga, focusing in on the areas I have worked on to allow the body to start repairing itself and calming the nervous system.

We are so lucky to live in a time where there are huge amounts of free yoga practices online that you can do in the comfort of your own home. All you need is a yoga mat, and some practices don't even require that. If you want a place to start, I can't recommend "Yoga with Adriene" enough. Her positive, relaxed approach is what I like to use as a contrast to the hard intense exercises I do. She also has videos for almost everything you can think of. There are videos for when you are ill, tired, aching, or have been running or cycling; there are also more challenging ones where you can work up a sweat. The choice is yours. I encourage you to give it a go and find a style that suits you.

I rotate my morning exercise between *qigong* (pronounced *chee-gong*), which translates to "energy work," and yoga. Originating in China five thousand years ago, qigong uses slow movements to move energy (qi) around the body and get rid of stagnant and negative energy, replenishing it with good, positive qi. Think of it like a phone that you plug in for a charge. There are numerous studies that show this can be beneficial for health, and you don't need any equipment for it. Again, there are plenty of free videos on YouTube. I recommend the Qi Tribe channel run by my friend and qigong mentor, Jamie Hughes.

So, there are my top five stress-busters. Don't feel you need to do them all. I started with meditation and breathing; two years later, I added gratitude, and another year later I committed myself regularly to yoga. The total amount of time every day for all combined is often around thirty minutes, split over two or three parts of the day. Go love yourself! You are worth it!

What Matters in Your Life?

Most of us get on with our lives, day in, day out. But where are we going, what are we doing, and why? Sure, we may come up with some quick answers, but how many are so deep-rooted that you set it out at the beginning of every day? We are all individuals with different needs, and we all have deep-rooted values, whether we know it or not. When you do something you think is bad, it is your values that have told you that.

So how can we live a life more in tune with our values? Write them down and look at them every day. Who are you? How do you want to be remembered? If you said you want to be remembered as a kind person, do you think having that written down with some actions as guiding values would help you achieve it more days than not? Give it a go and think about why. If you want to lose weight, why? If you can nail down that reason and look at it daily, you are more likely to achieve it. If the answer is to be healthy, then ask why again. Drill down into your values. Here is an example taken from my personal mission statement (this is only a small part of it):

My mission is to encourage people to be the best version of themselves. I will do this through being a good husband, son, brother, uncle, manager, colleague, and employee. To do that, I need to be the best person I can be. I will do this through:

- being kind to myself and others
- being loving to my friends and family
- getting stronger mentally and physically by eating healthy food, exercise, mediation and exercising my brain
- believing in myself

So, if you are one of the millions of people who wants to get healthier, know why. What motivates you? Do you want to be healthy so you can be active with your children, partner, or friends? Maybe you want to feel better in yourself or have a better quality of life?

Try creating your own vision statement by asking yourself the following questions:

- What is my mission in life?
- Why do I want to do that?
- What would that bring me?
- How will I do it?

Only you can answer these questions. Create your vision statement and look at it every day to remind you of who you are. If being healthy or eating more plant-based food doesn't pop up in your values, that is fine. Live your life. But if it does, and you have bounced from diet to diet, using this as a map will help you get to where you want to be and make the choices that matter to you. If they matter, then they are more likely to stick.

Ditch the Diet

Diets don't work. Fact! There is a lot of research that shows diets for weight loss often have the opposite effect, and people end up putting on more weight. You can't keep on eating less; it can't last. Your body needs fuel, not starvation. A plant-based lifestyle is a great way to manage your weight in a healthy way. If you eat enough of the right things, you are getting plenty of fibre that keeps you fuller for longer. Also, you are getting nutrition that your body needs.

Vitamins and minerals are essential, and the body has always gotten this through food. These days, a lot of food is devoid of it, especially processed food and fast food. Have you ever had processed or fast food and been hungry not long after, despite consuming lots of calories? That is because your body needs nutrients. If it doesn't get them in the food you just gave your body, it will ask for more food.

This is where people get in a cycle—constantly eating because their bodies are saying they want nutrient-dense food and they are providing nutrient-devoid food. So their bodies just keep asking for more. The recipes in this book are packed full of nutrients that will help tell your body you are full.

Caption – From saying life is good to living a good life

If you are looking to lose body fat, then I have a secret weapon for you. It is called intermittent fasting. One of the reasons people can struggle to lose fat in the body is that it is processing food most of the time. If your body is processing food, it can't do (or can't do as effectively) many of the amazing things a body can do, including healing and regeneration of the body and brain. If there is no food for it to process, then it goes looking for the next best thing: body fat!

Multiple scientific studies have shown how good intermittent fasting is for the brain and body. In fact, you may find you operate better without food in your body. So it seems breakfast *isn't* the most important meal of the day.

The best amount of time to fast is for fourteen to sixteen hours. The easy way to do this is to start from your last meal of the day and go fourteen to sixteen hours without consuming any calories. You should also be asleep for half of this time. I tend to eat my last meal at around eight at night and then eat again at noon the next day. The first time I did it, I was surprised at how easy it was, and I am sure you will be too.

So if you start at lunchtime, how many meals do you eat? The same as you would normally to get to your calorie target. That could be two big meals and a few snacks, or in my case three meals and two snacks (one for my wife). If you are trying to have a calorie deficit, this can really help. Just make sure you are getting enough nutrients in your body to give it what it needs (which can be hard over two meals).

There is a free app called the Daily Dozen by Dr Michael Greger which helps you check if you have eaten enough of the right foods for optimum health:

- 3 servings of beans (including chickpeas, peas, and lentils; hummus counts)
- 1 portion of berries
- 3 portions of other fruit
- 1 cruciferous vegetable (bok choy; broccoli, including broccoli sprouts; cabbage; and cauliflower)
- 2 portions of greens (rocket, spinach, kale, chard)
- 2 portions of other vegetables
- 1 portion of ground flaxseed
- 1 portion of nuts
- 1 serving of spices (chilli, garlic, ginger, turmeric, etc.)
- 3 portions of whole grains (oats, whole-wheat pasta, quinoa, brown rice, wholegrain bread, popcorn)
- vitamin B_{12} (more info in FAQs)
- vitamin D

If you are hungry, I would say eat something and take it from the list above.

Our stomachs are an amazing and complex part of our bodies. Amazingly, 90 per cent of the body's serotonin is produced in the digestive tract. Serotonin is known as the happy chemical and has a massive impact on happiness and well-being.

Get Active and Have Fun!

Being active is so important to a healthy life. No matter what state of health you are in, there is likely something you can do. Walking is a great place to start. If you don't walk at all, try going out for ten minutes and then increase it. Walk to the shops instead of driving. Take a walk at lunchtime. Not only does walking get you outside and embracing nature, it offers opportunities to relax by listening to music, or you can learn from or be entertained by a podcast.

If you aren't very active, I recommend you get an activity tracker. Find out what your current level of activity is and try to increase it.

Yoga is also a great activity to get you started and help build strength. If you have a decent level of fitness from walking and yoga, you can try doing workouts at home using resistance bands, your own body weight, or free weights. You don't need to go to the gym to get a good workout. Doing workouts that work on strength and mobility will help you so much now and later in life. It is never too late to start.

Once again, YouTube has loads of free videos you can give a go, and there are free Android and iOS apps too. If you have any concern over what level of physical activity is right for you, ask your doctor. Doctors will always be able to advise you on staying active safely.

Finally, have fun. If all of the above sounds like too much hard work, then ask yourself what you can do to create a sense of play. Dance, or reignite those tennis or badminton skills? Life is to be lived and enjoyed. Before you start your workout, always ask yourself how you can make it fun.

Sleep

One of the most important essentials for a healthy life is sleep. A consistent routine helps so much, and if you are getting enough sleep during the week, you won't need extra sleep at the weekend. A minimum of seven hours of sleep is what you should be aiming for.

This does not translate to seven hours in bed. The amount of time you spend in a state of disturbed sleep is quite high, so aim to be in bed somewhere between eight and nine hours. It may seem tough at first if you have spent most of your life going to bed late, but it won't take long for your body to adapt. Eventually, your body will thank you for the extra sleep through increased vitality and mood. If you are currently only spending seven hours in bed, increasing this by one or two hours is the equivalent of sleeping an extra five or ten hours during the week alone! When the weekend comes, you will feel refreshed and ready to have fun.

A quiet dark room is optimal for a good night's sleep. If this is not possible for you (due to street lights or a busy neighbourhood, for example), you can invest in an eye mask or blackout curtains and earplugs. These will greatly increase the quality of your sleep, and you will have more energy to go out and crush your goals.

Too much caffeine in your body can also disrupt the quality of your sleep. I cut off consumption of caffeinated products (pretty much just coffee) nine or ten hours before I plan on sleeping. You might believe you can sleep well enough having caffeine later in the day, but your deep sleep and REM sleep are likely to be affected without you realising. I have found a meditation practice also helps my sleep latency and quality.

To help you get started with planting the way to *your* success, I have created some videos to support you. Visit jamiebeets.com/BTL to access these for free.

Why Eat a Plant-Based Diet?

There are a number of reasons listed below. Feel free to go straight to the one that resonates with you the most.

Improved Health

This was my reason for moving to a plant-based diet. I had absolutely no idea of the health impact it could have. A whole-food (think whole grains) plant-based diet not only prevents heart disease and type 2 diabetes, it can actually reverse them! It is therefore more effective than prescription drugs. A whole-food plant-based diet has also been shown to have a significant effect on reducing a range of cancers and chronic diseases, including breast and prostate cancer. Finally, it considerably reduces your chances of getting Parkinson's or Alzheimer's. The diseases I have mentioned are just a few that a plant-based diet has an impact on. For more information on the health benefits of a plant-based diet, check out nutritionfacts.org.

Fitness and Recovery

Athletes on a plant-based diet say they are able to recover more quickly, have more energy, gain lean muscle mass faster, and have more strength. That's all after ditching meat and dairy.

Where do they get their protein from? Read the FAQs section later in this introduction. I have used a plant-based diet to get fitter, and I can say I am the fittest I have ever been.

There are a number of athletes who prove on a daily basis that you don't only survive on a plant-based diet, you thrive. Novak Djokovic, Lewis Hamilton, and Lionel Messi all choose plants over meat. So does Patrik Baboumian, who holds the world record for a yoke walk, carrying 560 kilograms for twenty-eight seconds!

Weight Loss

If you like eating, you are in the right place. A whole-food plant-based diet is lower in calories and more nutrient-dense than a standard Western diet. This means you are likely to eat more food to get to your target calorie intake. If you are looking to lose fat, this is the perfect diet, as you will be able to eat tasty food that may seem naughty but is actually doing you good.

I have said *lose fat* rather than *lose weight*, as *weight* can be misleading. Water and muscle are all part of your weight and are essential. Even if I don't look it, my BMI puts me at overweight due to my muscle mass. I know I am not overweight from two things: one is having a scale that measures body fat, and the other is looking in the mirror! Even if you don't have a scale that measures body fat, just look in the mirror. It will tell you more than an ordinary scale can.

Saving the Planet

Farming of livestock and grains to feed livestock is rapidly expanding. As a result, deforestation is commonplace around the globe. This is causing massive damage to the ecosystem and reducing the number of trees that can turn CO_2 into oxygen. Seeing the Amazon rainforest on fire is almost like seeing our own lungs on fire.

Our current way of eating large amounts of meat is crippling the planet, and without a major change, it will only get worse. The farming of plants uses drastically less water, carbon emission, and land. It presents the only way to stop the damage that has been done. Let's heal the Earth together!

Saving Money

You likely already eat plenty of grains in rice, pasta, and bread. If you eat a good amount of vegetables, that will continue or increase. Meat often gets replaced by legumes. Tofu, tempeh, beans, lentils, and chickpeas are all staple ingredients in this book. You can pick up a tin of chickpeas for less than 40p! I am pretty sure the legumes you will start eating will cost considerably less than the meat you have been buying. So the question is, what will you do with all that money you are saving?

Saving Animals

In the UK, approximately 2.6 million cows, 10 million pigs, 14.5 million sheep, 80 million fish, and 950 million birds are slaughtered every year to feed us. Knowing that we don't need animal protein to live a fit and healthy life begs the question: why are we taking away so many lives?

FAQs

Q: Will I get enough protein on a plant-based diet?

A: Yes, you will, especially by eating the recipes from this book, which I have designed for active people. If you are unsure, feel free to use a macro nutrient checking app. Not only have I lost body fat since eating a plant-based diet, I have increased my lean muscle mass.

In some recipes, I have listed protein powder as an optional extra. You don't need it, but if you are looking to get extra protein because of your nutrition goals, you can use a plant-based protein supplement. I really like using supplements from Vivo Life. Not only do their products taste great, their ingredients are 100 per cent plant-based. They are also free from additives, preservatives, colours, fillers, and binders, and use sustainable organic ingredients.

Q: Won't I be hungry?

A: Definitely not. The increased amount of fibre you will naturally get on a plant-based diet keeps you fuller for longer. I've found that my cravings for something to nibble on in the evenings no longer exists—unless I have expended a huge number of calories, in which case, I will make a simple nice cream.

Q: Will I get enough iron and calcium if I am not eating meat or dairy?

A: Brace yourself: You will probably get more iron and calcium, along with all the other amazing vitamins and nutrients you are getting from a plant-based diet. You'll also be able to absorb more iron and calcium.

Q: What about vitamin B_{12}, as you can only get that from meat?

A: There is a lot of hullabaloo around B_{12}. This vitamin is found in dirt! If we lived two hundred years ago, we would be getting it from water (from a well) and from vegetables that would have a bit of dirt on them. Now, with pesticides so commonly used in farming, we need to scrub the life and dirt from vegetables. We are living in an increasingly sterile world which does not support B_{12}, so we need to find another source, as do a lot of animals, through a supplement.

It is estimated that 90 per cent of B_{12} supplements go to animals, which is how it ends up in the food chain. I take a B_{12} supplement that is combined with a few other vitamins (including D) and probiotics every other day, although I'm not worried if I forget, as I know I am getting plenty of vitamins through my food. If you plan on switching your diet to completely plant-based, then I recommend you get a B_{12} supplement. If not, then you may be getting enough from meat and dairy. But even meat eaters can be B_{12} deficient!

Q: What about omega 3?

A: This one is a bit more complicated. Omega 3 is called an alpha-linoleic acid (ALA). Chia seeds, flaxseed, and sunflower seeds (which are all used in my recipes) are great sources of ALA. Your body can convert that ALA into other omega 3 acids, including eicosapentaenoic acid (EPA) and docosahexaenoic Acid (DHA). However, our bodies are all different and conversion can come at different rates with different people.

Without having a test to find out, it is best to take a vegan omega 3 supplement (make sure it's vegan). As with B_{12}, I take an omega 3 supplement every other day. Before becoming plant-based, I probably didn't have enough omega 3 in my diet. Now I probably do, but I won't take that chance and so take the supplement. I get my B_{12} as part of a multi nutrient from Vivo Life as well as their omega 3 oil.

Q: Will I need special ingredients?

A: Not a lot. The only ingredients you are unlikely to have already are flaxseed, chia seeds, cacao, and maca, which are easily available in most supermarkets. Another is nutritional yeast, which you can buy in some supermarkets or your local health store. A mixture of frozen fruit is also helpful.

Q: Isn't it more expensive?

A: It depends on how much meat and dairy you are consuming. Generally, it should be cheaper, as seeds, nuts, and legumes are all cheaper per portion than meat and dairy. Tempeh and tofu are likely to be the most expensive products and can replace a meat protein. A portion will cost around £1 to £1.50. Plant-based milk is likely to be more expensive, but that's it.

Q: *How do I know if something is vegan?*

A: It's unlikely to have a vegan sign; it's more likely to say *vegetarian* or have a vegetarian symbol. So the best way to check is to look at the ingredients on the back and see what is in bold as an allergen. Egg and dairy will show up there.

Q: *Does soya increase levels of oestrogen?*

A: Nope, this is a myth. Soya has phytoestrogens, which do not change testosterone levels in men. In fact, according to nutrionfacts.org, phytoestrogens appear to be helpful in the prevention of diabetes and cancers of the colon, liver, brain, breast, ovaries, and skin.

Q: *Won't the food be boring?*

A: Far from it. Just try the recipes in this book. If you have had a bad experience with plant-based dishes, think about which seasonings were used. How would an unseasoned piece of boiled chicken taste? Probably similar to an unseasoned piece of tofu. It's the seasonings that can make or break it.

Q: *How do I start?*

A: Don't feel you need to go in 100 per cent. Just starting off with one meal a week is a great way to go. Have a read and see where you want to start. Highlight the recipes you want to give a go. Three of the easiest are Porridge with Nice Cream, Spanish Chickpeas on Toast, and Creamy Sun-Dried Tomato Pasta. You will spend more time cleaning up than cooking!

Ingredients and Hacks

There are a few ingredients that might be new to you. Below is a bit of guidance on what they are, where you get them and why they are so good for you:

- **Flaxseed (also known as linseed)**
  You can pick this up in most supermarkets. It needs to be ground to be digested properly. But try not to buy it preground, as it can lose its nutritional value quickly. I like to grind enough to fill a small pot once a week. Flaxseed helps fight cancer, including breast and prostate, and also helps control cholesterol and blood sugar levels. Try to get one tablespoon of ground flaxseed in your diet every day.

- **Nutritional yeast**

  You can pick this up in quite a few supermarkets or health shops. This is your cheesy saviour for sauces, especially mac 'n' cheez. It is high in protein and most often fortified with vitamin B$_{12}$.

- **Broccoli sprouts**

  A few supermarkets have started selling these; however, I grow my own, and it is really easy to do. A twelve-gram serving counts as your daily cruciferous vegetable intake and is more nutrient-dense than a fully grown head of broccoli. The sprouts are light in taste, and a serving can easily be added to a lot of savoury dishes and salads.

And here's a kitchen hack I find useful: Get a good box grater, and never chop garlic or ginger again. Just use the fine side for garlic and medium for ginger. Effortless perfectly chopped garlic and ginger can be yours!

About the Recipes

The recipes in this book have been designed to be nutritious, tasty, easy, and in most cases, quick (between ten and thirty minutes). My hope is you will be able to see that plant-based food can be tasty. You don't have to spend hours in the kitchen, and a few tools and skills can go a long way and save time.

Don't feel that if you are missing some of the ingredients for a recipe, you cannot do it. Play around with what you have available. An example is the tempeh "chorizo" quesadilla. If you can't get either of the chilli powders, just use what chilli sauce you have in your cupboard.

The size of the portions can be adapted, too, to suit your health goals. Using a food-tracking app can help you see how many calories you are getting, and you can adjust the portions of your meals to suit you. Maybe you want less peanut butter, less rice, or less fruit. Food-tracking apps are great for seeing your macro intake (protein, carbohydrates, and fat). Depending on what you are doing or working towards, this can help refine what you are eating. This of course is optional, but it is really useful when you start a new diet. Find what works for you.

All the recipes have a good amount of carbohydrates and fats in them. Despite what social media "experts" may tell you, carbs or fat are not bad for you—well, not on a whole-food plant-based diet. Your body needs carbs, fat, and protein, so why deny it?

The recipes in this book are broken down into three sections: breakfasts; lunches, mains, and sides; and desserts and sweet treats. Feel free to play around with the format. If you would prefer to have one of the sweet treats as breakfast or one of the breakfasts as a snack or a sweet treat, as long as it fits into your calories for the day, by all means, go ahead.

Most of the recipes in this book are at around the 600-calorie mark. However, if you are monitoring your caloric intake, I advise you to do the calculations on an online calculator before you cook. Many of the recipes are easy to double or quadruple, and freezing is often an easy way to make foods last longer, especially things like daal and chilli. Feel free to mix up the meals at different times of the day while keeping in mind a healthy and balanced diet. Although I might love to eat porridge and nice cream or smoothie bowls for every meal, I know this would not be nutritionally complete, even if it was very tasty!

Moving onto a plant-based diet is a journey that has many routes to choose from. There is no perfect path; you need to find the one that is right for you. Some people can instantly switch, while others might only be able to incorporate one meal a week. If you can only do one meal, good for you! Remember the difference that one meal is making to your body, health, and planet. Each step forward is in the right direction. If it takes one day, ten weeks, or ten years, it doesn't matter. Doing the best you can do today is what matters. Having your values written down will really help guide you.

Finally, focus on a positive, not a negative. If you tell yourself you won't eat meat, then guess what? You are going to want meat! You are choosing plants as your food source. If you wake up one day and need a steak, then have it. Denying yourself only leads to distrustful behaviour. Make your food choices from your heart, where your values lie.

To help with this, write out a weekly meal plan (download a template at jamiebeets.com). Knowing what you are eating and when will help your shopping and make it less likely that you will stray from the path. You can help plan for busy days by making extra food the day before so you can just come home and reheat. My preferred time to do my list is at the weekend with a cup of coffee.

Go plant your way to a happier and healthier you!

Jamie

BREAKFAST

Start your day in a vibrant way

Granola

This is great to have in the house. You can eat it for breakfast with some yoghurt (I like vanilla soy yoghurt) and plenty of berries or other fruit; sprinkled on top of a smoothie bowl; or as a little snack like trail mix. When having it as a breakfast I have somewhere between 70–100 grams with around 150 grams of yoghurt and 150 grams mixed berries. This recipe is enough to fill two large jars and should last at least a month, but it is likely you will have eaten it all by then!

Makes 30–40 portions

3 tablespoons coconut oil
270 grams mixed nuts
240 grams oats
350 grams mixed seeds
3 tablespoons maple syrup
1 tablespoon ground cinnamon
100 grams raisins
50 grams coconut flakes
120 grams dried banana chips

1. Preheat oven to 160°C. Add coconut oil to a large, deep baking tray (or use 2 smaller trays) and allow to melt.

2. Meanwhile, roughly chop nuts (you could do this in a food processor, but chopping by hand gives bigger pieces). Add to the baking tray along with oats, seeds, syrup, and cinnamon. Mix thoroughly.

3. Bake for 30–40 minutes, stirring every 10 minutes. You want the granola to be nicely toasted but not burnt. When the granola has finished in the oven, add the raisins, coconut flakes, and banana chips.

4. When granola has cooled, store in an airtight container or jar.

PBJ Smoothie Bowl

This is my go-to pre-exercise meal. With plenty of fruits, oats, and healthy fats, it will really keep you going. The longer you plan on working out, the more peanut butter, dates, and chia seeds you can add. This can come up as quite dense calorie-wise, but if you are about to do a three-hour bike ride, that is what you need, so adjust the amount as required. You can also add some protein powder if you need it, although I wouldn't recommend more than one scoop.

The chia seeds are the backbone to this endurance breakfast. Chia seeds are a great source of protein, fat, and fibre, and will provide a long slow release of energy. They have been used for thousands of years in the Americas, with the Mayans and Aztecs using them for endurance in battle or running. The word *chia* translates to "strength" in Mayan.

Serves 1

160–200 millilitres water or coconut water, more if needed
160 grams mixed frozen berries
1 banana
1–3 dates
15 grams oats
5 grams ground linseed/flaxseed
protein powder (optional)
10–30 grams chia seeds
peanut butter (for serving)
granola (for serving)
handful of fresh berries (for serving)

1. In a blender, combine water, berries, banana, dates, oats, linseed/flaxseed, and protein powder (if using). Blitz until smooth, adding more liquid if required.

2. Transfer to a bowl and stir in chia seeds. Leave in the fridge for around 10 minutes, allowing chia seeds to thicken the mixture up.

3. Serve with peanut butter (amount depending on what you are doing), a spoonful of granola, and fresh berries on top. Enjoy, then go out and win!

Porridge with Nice Cream

This isn't my invention (as far as I'm aware, it came from Ferdinand Beck, aka *@vegainsfood* on Instagram), and I was a bit sceptical before making it. However, the combination of hot and cold is brilliant! It's perfect before or after exercise, but feel free to have it for lunch or dinner, too!

Nice cream is the healthy and vegan-friendly version of ice cream, made from blitzing frozen fruit and as little liquid as your blender can manage. I have included protein powder, but how much you put in is up to you and your dietary requirements. If you do, you can reduce the amount of oats, which are one of the main sources of protein in this recipe.

Serves 1

Porridge:
40–100 grams oats
10 grams ground flaxseed
1/2 teaspoon cacao powder
1/2 teaspoon maca powder
pinch of salt
protein powder (optional)
maple syrup to taste (optional)

Nice cream:
200–300 grams mixed frozen berries (a mixture including blueberries)
1/2–1 frozen banana
140–160 millilitres plant based milk
protein powder (optional)

For serving:
1 teaspoon–1 tablespoon nut butter
1 tablespoon granola
handful of berries

1. Start a kettle of water boiling.

2. **Make the porridge**: In a bowl, combine all ingredients. Cover with boiling water and mix well, adding more water if desired.

3. **Make the nice cream:** In a blender or food processor, combine all ingredients. Blend until smooth. You might need to add a little extra milk depending on the power of your blender.

4. **Serve:** Add the porridge to a large bowl, trying to keep it to one side. Pour the nice cream on the other side. Top with nut butter, granola, and berries. Eat while porridge is still warm and nice cream is still cold.

PBJ Pancakes

PBJ (peanut butter and jam) and pancakes are two of my favourite things, so it made sense to put them together, although I have replaced jam with fruit. I have this most weekends before going to the gym.

Serves 2

120 grams oats
15 grams ground linseed
1 banana
1 teaspoon baking powder
pinch of salt
1 teaspoon coconut oil
peanut butter
200 grams mixed berries
maple syrup (optional)

1. In a blender, blitz oats until they become a flour. Add linseed, banana, 240 millilitres water, baking powder, and salt. Blend until smooth; you want a thick cream-like consistency. If too thick, add a little more water. Set aside for 10 minutes.

2. In a nonstick frying pan, heat coconut oil over medium-high heat. Preheat oven on the lowest setting with a large plate inside.

3. Add a heaped tablespoon of batter to pan (I can normally get 3 to 4 pancakes in on one go). Give it 3–4 minutes, then flip; the pancake should be starting to brown nicely. Cook for another 3–4 minutes and then place on the plate in the oven to keep warm while you finish up the rest of the mix.

4. When all cooked, stack pancakes with a teaspoon of peanut butter and a dessert spoon of berries each. Continue until you have 2 pancake stacks, then serve. You can add a little drizzle of maple syrup, if you like.

Tofu Scramble

I was never much for scrambled eggs, but I knew how to make a good batch. Before moving to a plant-based diet, I wasn't a fan of tofu either. A tofu scramble, on the other hand, is a great breakfast, lunch, or dinner. You could also have it as a side.

Serves 2

1 tablespoon olive oil
1 onion, roughly chopped
1 red pepper, roughly chopped
1 tomato, roughly chopped
large handful mushrooms, sliced
1 garlic clove, finely chopped
1 chili, roughly chopped (optional)
big pinch of salt
280 grams extra-firm tofu, drained and squeezed dry
pinch of turmeric
pinch of black pepper
large handful of spinach
2 slices sourdough bread
small bunch coriander, chopped (optional)
1 avocado, sliced
chili sauce, for serving

1. In a large frying pan, heat olive oil over medium-high heat. Add onion, red pepper, tomato, mushrooms, garlic, chili, and salt. Cook for 5 minutes. All the veg should be soft, with a little moisture left in the pan.

2. When the veg is soft, crumble the tofu in your hands and into the pan (so that it has the texture of scrambled egg). Add turmeric and pepper. Stir regularly and cook for about 2 minutes. Add spinach to pan.

3. Toast the bread.

4. When spinach has wilted, add coriander, season and stir. Plate up the toast, then evenly share the tofu scramble. Add the sliced avocado and serve with your favourite chili sauce.

Full English Breakfast

What to do when you have a hangover and would normally have a greasy fry-up? Have no fear, a full English breakfast is here! Not only does this taste great, fill you up, and cure your hangover (no guarantees), it is giving you good nutrition to start your day.

There are a whole host of vegan sausages on the market, some aimed at tasting more like vegetables, others more like meat. I will leave the choice to you. Don't worry about the protein content from the sausage, as the toast, tofu, and beans will have you covered.

Serves 2

plant-based sausages of your choice
2 large or 4–6 small tomatoes, cut in half
4 large mushrooms, roughly sliced
salt
2 teaspoons coconut oil, divided
1 small white onion, finely chopped
1/2 teaspoon mustard powder
1/2 teaspoon of your preferred seasoning
(such as BBQ or Cajun)
1/2 teaspoon smoked paprika

1 tin cannellini beans, drained
tomato passata
1 tablespoon BBQ sauce
280 grams extra-firm tofu, drained and
squeezed dry
pinch of turmeric
handful of baby spinach leaves
1 tablespoon nutritional yeast
1–2 slices of bread per person

1. Preheat oven to 200°C. Place sausages, tomatoes, and mushrooms on a baking tray with a good pinch of salt on the tomatoes and mushrooms. Place in the oven and cook to the sausage packet instructions.

2. In a small saucepan, heat 1 teaspoon coconut oil over medium heat. Add onion and cook until soft, about 4 minutes.

3. Add mustard powder, preferred seasoning, and paprika. Stir and cook for 30 seconds.

4. Add drained beans and then enough passata to cover the beans. Add the BBQ sauce. Bring to a simmer, then put the heat to low while you finish everything else.

5. In a large frying pan, heat remaining 1 teaspoon coconut oil over medium heat. Crumble in the tofu and stir. Add turmeric, spinach, and nutritional yeast. Stir and reduce the heat to low.

6. When sausages have a couple of minutes left, toast your bread. Once the sausages are done, plate everything up as you would like and say goodbye to the hangover.

Overnight Oats

This couldn't be easier and is perfect for a breakfast to take to work if you are intermittent fasting. Just stick it in a plastic container.

Serves 1

60–100 grams oats
10 grams ground flaxseed
10 grams chia seeds
1/2 teaspoon maca (optional)
1/2 teaspoon cacao
200–250 millilitres plant-based milk
160 grams mixed berries, including blueberries (frozen is fine)
1 teaspoon maple syrup (optional)
protein powder (optional)

1. In a bowl or lunch box with a lid, mix the oats, flaxseed, chia seeds, maca, protein powder (if using) and cacao with the milk.

2. Top with mixed berries and maple syrup. Cover and put in the fridge overnight (or at least 6 hours).

Autumn Overnight Oats

This is great any time of year, but the spices really remind me of autumn and winter. If you don't fancy eating it cold, feel free to heat it up in the microwave or cook as you would a normal porridge, adding the apple at the end.

Serves 1

50–100 grams oats
200–300 millilitres plant-based milk (depending on how much oats you use)
10 grams ground flaxseed
1 teaspoon maca powder
1/2 teaspoon cinnamon
1/4 teaspoon ground ginger
1/4 teaspoon nutmeg
pinch of salt
1 medium carrot, peeled and grated
1 apple, cored and roughly chopped
1 tablespoon raisins
1 teaspoon maple syrup (optional)
protein powder (optional)

In a bowl or lunch box with a lid, combine all the ingredients and put in the fridge overnight. If making as a porridge, leave the apple and maple syrup to add at the end.

Brainberry Smoothie

This will give your brain and body a boost. The healthy fats in this smoothie mean certain vitamins are absorbed better by the body. I use this for my multivitamin and omega 3 source (from Vivo Life), as not only does it have your vitamins covered, it has lion's mane mushroom and gotu kola, both of which help with brain function and prevent cognitive decline. On top of that, you have blueberries and walnuts, which have been found to improve brain function and improve memory.

Serves 1

80 grams blueberries
1 banana
1 date
1/2 medium avocado
15 grams walnuts
1 heaped teaspoon cacao powder
1/2 teaspoon spirulina (optional)
1 serving Vivo Life Thrive multi-nutrient
1 serving omega 3 supplement
1/2 scoop Vivo Life protein powder (optional)
300 millilitres water

Put everything in a blender and blitz till smooth. Then go out and crush your goals!

Chocolate Hazelnut Butter with Berries on Sourdough Toast

This is a much healthier take on the popular chocolate hazelnut spread found on many families' breakfast tables. Unlike the shop-bought version, this contains no added sugars, milk, or palm oils. You can buy vegan versions in some shops, but to make it healthier, you can make your own. You need a good blender for this nut butter, but it will come together quickly.

Serves 1

Chocolate hazelnut butter:
240 grams hazelnuts (blanched hazelnuts make it easier)
80 millilitres plant-based milk
2 tablespoons maple syrup
2 tablespoons cacao powder
pinch of salt

Toast:
1 piece sourdough bread
40–50 grams chocolate hazelnut butter
1 banana, cut into 1-centimetre slices (optional)
150 grams mixed berries
couple of spoons of vanilla soya yoghurt

Make the chocolate hazelnut butter:

1. Preheat oven to 170°C.

2. Spread hazelnuts on a baking sheet. Roast for 10 minutes or until lightly golden. Allow to cool for at least 30 minutes.

3. If your hazelnuts have skins on, place the nuts in a box and shake vigorously to make it easier to take the skin off. Once clean, place roasted nuts in a blender and blitz for 20 seconds, allowing to rest 1 minute before repeating the process, until the mixture is smooth and creamy. (If you are unlikely to finish the batch within a week, set aside half the ground hazelnuts to finish another time, as the milk you are adding will have a limited use-by time. They can be stored in a cupboard.)

4. Add remaining ingredients and blitz again until smooth and creamy. Place in a clean jar or bowl.

Prepare the toast:

5. Toast the sourdough under the grill.

6. Serve toasted bread on a plate, adding the hazelnut butter, banana (if using), and berries, and topping off with yoghurt.

Black Forest Gat—oh!

As a child of the eighties, I have a special place in my heart for Black Forest gateau. This smoothie bowl has all the flavour of the eighties classic but is full of great nutrients. Give this a go! If you don't want to use protein powder, add 30–40 grams of oats and an extra teaspoon of nut butter.

Serves 1

Gateau:
120 grams frozen cherries (plus more for serving)
80 grams frozen blueberries (plus more for serving)
1 banana (preferably frozen)
1 large medjool date
1 scoop chocolate-flavoured protein (optional)
1 tablespoon chia seeds
1 tablespoon ground flax
1–2 teaspoons cacao
100 millilitres plant-based milk

For serving:
granola
toasted coconut flakes
nut butter (chocolate hazelnut butter works really well here)
seeds

1. **Make the gateau:** In a high-powered blender, combine all the ingredients except the ones for serving and blend until smooth and thick, adding more plant-based milk if needed.

2. **Serve:** Transfer to a bowl, add toppings of your choice (you could go all out with whipped coconut cream!), and top with berries and cherries.

PBJ on Sweet Potato Toast

It may sound mad, but this is great for a preworkout breakfast—or lunch. Sweet potatoes contain many vitamins, including B_6, C, and D (sunshine!), and are full of potassium and magnesium. I have paired the sweet potatoes with one of my favourite combos: peanut butter and jam. Making your own jam is really easy. All you need is frozen or fresh berries and chia seeds.

Serves 2

200 grams mixed berries, frozen or fresh
20 grams chia seeds
1 large sweet potato, cut into 1-centimetre slices (skin on)
peanut butter or almond butter
1 banana, sliced (optional)
mixed seeds (optional)

1. Preheat oven to 220°C. If berries are frozen, defrost in the microwave on medium heat.

2. Mash up berries with a fork, stir in the chia seeds, mix well, and set aside.

3. Place sweet potato slices on a nonstick tray. Roast until cooked, 15–20 minutes.

4. Once sweet potatoes are cooked, plate up. Top the slices with remaining ingredients whichever way you like, finishing with the mixed seeds if you are using them.

French Toast

Oh yes, you can have French toast on a plant-based diet! For me, this is Sunday mornings. I have included two options, one with protein powder (which thickens it) and one without that also adds protein and healthy fats.

Serves 2

Batter:

Option 1

200 millilitres plant-based milk or water

70 grams protein powder (strawberry and vanilla work really well here)

10 grams ground flaxseed

Option 2

285 millilitres plant-based milk or water

30 grams cashews soaked in boiled water for 10 minutes, then drained

20 grams flaxseed

Toast:

2–3 teaspoons coconut oil

2–4 slices bread (sourdough is great), cut in half

For serving:

150 grams of your favourite plant-based yoghurt

1 banana (optional)

300–400 grams mixed berries

4 teaspoons almond butter

maple syrup (optional)

sprinkling of mixed seeds, granola, or trail mix (optional)

Make the batter:

1. In a blender or food processor, combine ingredients for option 1 or 2. Use a little less liquid to start off, as it is easier to add liquid than to take it away. You want the texture to be like a thick custard. Your finger should leave a trail if you put your finger through it. If too thick, add a little extra milk. If too runny, add a little extra flaxseed.

2. Transfer batter to a wide dish and set aside for 5 minutes. Turn the oven to its lowest setting and add a plate where you will keep the cooked toast warm.

3. **Cook the toast:**

4. In a large pan, heat 1 teaspoon coconut oil over medium-high heat. Dip bread halves in the batter mix, ensuring each is completely covered. Let any excess drip off before placing it in the hot pan. Repeat until the pan is full (for me, this could be half or a third of all the bread).

5. Cook 3–5 minutes on each side until batter is starting to go dark. You need to use your instinct and senses here, as if you check too early, you will end up with a creamy mess. Let the batter around the edges settle and start to crisp up. This should be a good indicator, but try to use your nose, eyes, and ears to tell if it's ready.

6. Once the toast is cooked, add it to a plate in the oven. Add another teaspoon of oil (if required) to pan and repeat until all of the toast is cooked.

Serve:

1. Plate up cooked toast with yoghurt, banana (if using), and berries before drizzling the almond butter over (and maple syrup, if using). Finish with seeds, granola, or trail mix, if desired. Serve and enjoy!

Sweet Potato Smoothie Bowl

This may sound odd but give it a go. If you like chocolate mousse, then imagine eating a massive bowl of it *and* knowing it's good for you. This is great after a workout or exercise, and you could even have it as a post-workout snack. You can adjust the amount of sweet potato and toppings to make it more or less calorific. You need to have prepared the sweet potato at least a few hours before.

Serves 1

125–200 grams sweet potato, halved
200–250 millilitres plant-based milk
50–100 grams frozen banana
50 grams frozen blueberries
1 medjool date
5 grams ground flaxseed
2 teaspoons cacao
1/2–1 teaspoon cinnamon
chocolate protein (optional)

Toppings:
almond butter or chocolate hazelnut butter
granola
60 grams mixed berries (I love Black Forest berry mix for this)

1. Place sweet potato in a bowl, cover, and microwave for 5–6 minutes. Allow to cool, then place in the fridge for at least a couple of hours.

2. When ready to eat, blend milk, sweet potato flesh, banana, blueberries, date, flaxseed, cacao, cinnamon, and chocolate protein (if using). Blend until smooth, adding more milk if required. You want a thick, mousse-like consistency.

3. Pour, then scrape into a bowl and add your choice of toppings. Enjoy!

Lunches, Mains and Sides

Nutritious and delicious! These dishes will have you thinking you are eating something naughty but they will leave you feeling energised and satiated.

Jerk Tempeh with Jamaican Rice and Beans

Tempeh, which can now be found in some supermarkets, is a great source of protein. It's made from slightly fermented soybeans and formed into a firm cake, giving it quite a meaty texture. Doesn't sound so appealing? Give it a go! It's great for BBQ, grilling, and pan-frying, and can become nice and crisp.

Tempeh is great at soaking up flavour, and jerk sauce is perfect for it, especially under the grill next to pineapple, peppers, and red onions. I have paired this with coconut rice and beans (or, as they say in Jamaica, peas).

Serves 2

Kebabs:
1 (200-gram) block tempeh, sliced into 1/2-centimetre slices
2 tablespoons jerk sauce
1/2 teaspoon jerk spice (optional)
pinch of salt
1 red pepper, cut into 2-centimetre wedges
2 small red onions, cut into 2-centimetre wedges
1/4–1/2 fresh pineapple, sliced into 2–3-centimetre squares

Rice:
120 grams wholegrain basmati rice, washed
200 millilitres coconut milk
60 millilitres water
1 tin black beans, drained and rinsed
1 sprig thyme
1 spring onion, smashed
1 chilli, kept whole, preferably Scotch bonnet (optional)
big pinch of salt
1/2 tsp jerk spice (optional)

Make the kebabs:

1. A few hours before cooking (or even the night before), marinate tempeh in jerk sauce, jerk spice, and salt, making sure tempeh is all covered.

2. When ready to cook, skewer tempeh, red pepper, onions, and pineapple in whatever order you want, but do two pieces of tempeh for each piece of the other ingredients.

Make the rice:

3. In a saucepan, combine rice ingredients. Bring to a simmer and cover to cook as per rice package guidance (often around 25–30 minutes).

4. Heat grill to medium-high. Alternatively, heat up the BBQ. Grill/BBQ skewers until they start to char (5–8 minutes per side). If there is any marinade left, you can brush this on.

5. Once rice is cooked, remove thyme, spring onion, and chilli.

6. Serve rice with cooked kebabs, on or off the skewer. Feel free to mix it all together.

Creamy Sun-Dried Tomato Pasta

This is so easy to make and great if you haven't got much time. It also uses only a few store cupboard staples. This is also delicious cold as a pasta salad. I prefer to use chickpea or lentil pasta, as it has a much higher amount of protein compared to regular pasta.

Serves 1, and easy to multiply

whole meal or chickpea/lentil pasta
30 grams cashews
garlic clove
80 grams frozen peas
80 grams frozen or tinned sweetcorn
handful of kale/spinach
4 sun-dried tomatoes
5 grams nutritional yeast (available from Holland and Barret or some supermarkets; tastes like cheese!)
pinch of salt

1. Boil the kettle and start cooking pasta. Cooking times vary depending on the pasta you use, check the packet for cooking times.

2. Cover cashews and garlic clove with some of the boiling water (around 90 millilitres).

3. When there is 4 minutes cooking time left on the pasta, add peas, sweetcorn, and kale (if using spinach, add at the end).

4. In a blender, combine cashews, garlic, and soaking water with sun-dried tomatoes, nutritional yeast, salt, and a bit of water (if required) to make it the consistency you want. Blitz until smooth and creamy, adding more water if necessary.

5. Drain the pasta and veg, add the sauce, and enjoy!

Caesar Salad

Before I moved to a plant-based diet, Caesar salad was one of my favourite dishes in the summer. Any Caesar salad craving is easily met by this plant-based version. The inclusion of seaweed flakes and miso gives it an umami flavour, with the added benefit of minerals and nutrients. Soak the cashews in water for an hour or two before making the salad. If you forget, just soak in hot water that has just boiled while you prepare the rest of the meal.

Serves 2

1 small cauliflower, sliced into steaks about 1-centimetre thick, cutting out the core
3 teaspoon melted coconut oil, divided
salt
150–200 grams bread, sliced into large croutons

1 tin chickpeas, rinsed and drained
1/2 head crispy lettuce (romaine is perfect for this), roughly sliced
2 tomatoes, roughly chopped
1/4 cucumber, halved and roughly sliced
120 grams cooked quinoa

Dressing:
40 grams soaked cashews
80 millilitres water
20 grams tahini
12 grams nutritional yeast, found in some supermarkets or health stores

1 garlic clove
juice of 1 lemon
1 teaspoon seaweed flakes (optional)
1 teaspoon white miso (optional)
3/4 teaspoon Dijon mustard

1. Heat oven to 200°C.

2. Place cauliflower slices on a baking tray with 1 teaspoon melted coconut oil. Season generously with salt (you can add any other spice mix you like), then put in the oven.

3. Place croutons on another baking tray with drained chickpeas. Coat with remaining 2 teaspoons coconut oil. Season with salt before putting in the oven. Both take around 15 minutes; just check every now and then. You are looking for the cauliflower to start browning and the croutons to be nice and crisp.

4. **Make the dressing:** Meanwhile, drain cashews, then place all dressing ingredients into a blender and blend until smooth. You can add a bit more water if you want the dressing runnier. Taste for seasoning, adding salt if required and some black pepper. Set aside.

5. In a large serving bowl, combine lettuce, tomatoes, cucumber, and quinoa.

6. Once the cauliflower, chickpeas, and croutons are ready, add to bowl, finishing off with dressing. Serve

Gallo Pinto

Gallo Pinto is the national dish of Costa Rica, made from rice and beans. You see it on every menu, and it can be eaten as a breakfast, lunch, dinner, or side. My version makes it incredibly healthy, with plenty of vegetables and fruit thrown in to make it a nutrient-dense meal. Even if the idea of it doesn't inspire you, I urge you to give it a go.

This can be made more quickly by using cooked rice, but the cooking of the rice in the beans and vegetable mix takes it to the next level. The simple salsa can be made while cooking the rice and beans, and it provides a fresh contrast to the deep and rich rice and beans. If you eat it over two days, I suggest you make half the amount of salsa and make it fresh each time you eat it.

Serves 4–6

Gallo pinto:
1 tablespoon olive oil
2 bell peppers, cut into 1-centimetre dice
2 medium white onions, finely chopped
2 tomatoes, roughly chopped
salt
3 cloves garlic, finely chopped
1 green chilli, finely chopped (seeds and membrane can be removed)
2 cups (240 millilitres) wild rice or brown basmati
2 cups water
1 vegetable stock cube
2 (400-gram) tins black beans, drained
1 fresh bay leaf

Salsa:
You can chop the vegetables as rough or fine as you like.
1 red onion, finely chopped
juice of 1 lime
salt
4 tomatoes, chopped
2 medium ripe avocados, diced
1 green chilli, chopped (optional)
handful of coriander, chopped

Make gallo pinto:

1. In a large saucepan, big enough to cook the rice, heat olive oil over medium heat. When oil is hot, add bell peppers, onions, tomatoes, and a big pinch of salt. Fry until soft and the onions have become translucent. Add garlic and chilli. Cook until fragrant and soft (about 1 minute).

2. Add rice to pan and mix well. Add 2 cups of water with the stock cube, black beans, bay leaf, and 2 teaspoons salt. Bring to a slow boil; cover, reduce heat to a simmer, and cook to the instructions on the rice packet. Check a couple of minutes before the time is up to make sure rice doesn't get too soft.

3. Once rice is cooked, take pan off the heat and set aside for 5 minutes, keeping it covered.

Make salsa:

4. While rice is cooking, in a medium bowl, combine onion with lime juice and a big pinch of salt. Mix thoroughly before adding tomatoes, avocados, chilli, and coriander. Taste to season, and set aside for flavours to come together.

Serve:

5. After rice has cooked, mix the gallo pinto thoroughly, check the seasoning, and add salt if required. Serve with a generous serving of the salsa on top.

Gochujang Tofu Bibimbap

What's *bibimbap*? It's a Korean mixed rice dish. Rather than the vegetables being added during cooking, bibimbap has vegetables added at the end so you get a mixture of textures and flavours. Although the ingredients list is long, this is really easy to pull together.

Gochujang is a Korean chilli paste you can pick up in some supermarkets; it's worth tracking down. If you can't get gochujang, just use your favourite chilli sauce. You can marinate the tofu for a few hours or overnight to add depth of flavour.

Serves 2

Marinade:
1 tablespoon gochujang sauce
1 tablespoon soy sauce
1/2 tablespoon sesame oil
1 clove garlic, finely grated
1 inch ginger, coarsely grated

Tofu and mushrooms:
225 grams extra-firm smoked tofu, cut into cubes
250 grams mushrooms, roughly chopped
1 teaspoon sesame oil
2 handfuls beansprouts
2 handfuls baby leaf spinach
couple big pinches of salt
1 tablespoon soy sauce

Sauce:
1 tablespoon gochujang sauce
1 tablespoon soy sauce
1 tablespoon sesame oil
1 tablespoon cider or any wine vinegar

For serving:
250 grams cooked wholegrain rice
2 carrots, sliced into 3-inch buttons
1/2 cucumber, sliced into 3-inch buttons
kimchi, about 1 tablespoon per person (but it's up to you)
4 spring onions, finely sliced
2 teaspoons sesame seeds

1. Heat oven to 200°C. Line a baking tray with foil (if you don't, you will be scrubbing it clean, even on a nonstick pan).

2. **Make marinade:** Mix all marinade ingredients together. Add tofu slices and soak, the longer the better.

3. **Cook tofu:** Add marinated tofu to prepared baking tray. Cook in oven until the tofu starts colouring and getting crisp, 10–15 minutes.

4. **Cook mushrooms**: In a large frying pan, cook mushrooms with sesame oil. Once mushrooms have started to colour, add beansprouts, spinach, salt, and soy sauce. Cover and cook until spinach has wilted and beansprouts are starting to soften.

5. **Make the sauce:** Mix everything together in a cup.

6. **Serve:** When tofu and mushrooms are almost done, heat up rice and split it between two bowls. Top with tofu, mushroom mixture, carrots, cucumber, kimchi, spring onions, and sesame seeds, then drizzle on the sauce and enjoy! Welcome to the world of Korean food!

Refried Beans Bagel

This is one of my go-to post-gym meals. Easy, quick, and very tasty with some chilli sauce on the side. You will feel full and nourished.

Serves 2

60 grams cashews
1 teaspoon olive oil
1 onion, roughly chopped
2–3 cloves garlic, finely grated
1 teaspoon cumin seeds
2 tins black beans, divided
1 tablespoon fajita spice
1 teaspoon dried oregano
2 bagels, halved
2 tablespoon nutritional yeast
1/2 spring onion (optional)
good pinch of salt
2 tomatoes, sliced
1 avocado, sliced
2 tablespoon broccoli sprouts (optional)
chilli sauce (I love a fruity habanero sauce with this)

1. In a kettle, boil a small amount of water. Place cashews in a mug and pour 80 millilitres of freshly boiled water over. Set aside until the end.

2. Preheat the grill.

3. In a large frying pan, heat olive oil over medium-high heat. Add onion, garlic, and cumin seeds. Fry until onions just start to colour.

4. Drain one tin of black beans and add to pan along with fajita spice and oregano.

5. Place remaining tin of beans, including water, in a blender and blitz quickly. Add to pan and cook, stirring frequently until beans have thickened up. Taste to season.

6. Stick bagels under the grill to toast.

7. In a clean blender, combine cashews with their soaking liquid, nutritional yeast, spring onion (if using), and salt, adding a little more water if required.

8. Once bagel is toasted, serve with bean mixture on top, followed by tomato slices, avocado slices, cashew mixture, and broccoli sprouts. Serve with your favourite chilli sauce.

Spanish Chickpeas on Toast

This is one of my favourite go-to lunches when I'm in a rush. It has over 35 grams of protein.

Serves 1 (but easy to double or quadruple)

2 slices wholemeal bread
1 (400-gram) tin chickpeas, drained
30 grams ground almonds
1 1/2 teaspoons smoked paprika
2 teaspoons vinegar (sherry, wine or cider)
1 small garlic clove
salt
1 tomato, sliced
1/2 avocado, sliced
broccoli sprouts (optional)
pepper

1. Stick bread in the toaster or under the grill.

2. Drain chickpeas and put into a blender or food processor with almonds, paprika, vinegar, garlic, and a good pinch of salt. Add some water and blend until smooth, adding more water if required.

3. Load chickpea mixture onto toast slices followed by tomato, avocado and broccoli sprouts. Finish off with salt and pepper.

Mac 'n' Cheez

I loved mac 'n' cheese as a kid. My dad would make it for me on a Saturday lunchtime. His twist was to use mustard powder, and I would finish it with salt and pepper. This version has the mustard, sneaks in three vegetables to boost nutrition, and uses cashews in place of cheese.

Serves 6

1 small butternut squash, cut into cubes (or buy frozen)
160 grams cashews, divided
1 small cauliflower, cut into large florets
500 grams macaroni (wholewheat if possible, or lentil/chickpea)
85 grams nutritional yeast, divided
pinch of garlic powder
salt
500 millilitres plant-based milk.
2 tablespoons cider or white wine vinegar
3 teaspoons mustard powder
350 grams peas

1. Halve squash, scoop out seeds, and microwave, covered, for 16 minutes or until flesh is soft.

2. While squash cooks, fill the kettle and bring to a boil. Soak 100 grams of the cashews in boiling water, then put the remaining water in a saucepan and add cauliflower. Simmer until tender.

3. Bring the kettle to a boil once again to cook the macaroni until just cooked.

4. While everything is cooking, make cashew parmesan by combining remaining 60 grams cashews, 70 grams of the nutritional yeast, garlic powder, and a pinch of salt in a food processor. Blitz until fine. Set aside.

5. Once everything is cooked, in a blender or food processor, combine cauliflower, squash, soaked and drained cashews, milk, vinegar, mustard powder, remaining 15 grams nutritional yeast, and a large pinch of salt to a blender or food processor (you may need to do this in two batches). Blend until mixture becomes a smooth creamy sauce. Taste to season, adding more salt, vinegar, or mustard to taste

6. Either microwave the peas for 3 minutes or briefly cook in any of the reserved cooking water.

7. Mix sauce with cooked macaroni and peas. Pour into a large baking tin or dish and top with cashew parmesan. Place under grill until golden. Serve with a green salad.

Quesadillas

Before moving to a plant-based diet, I loved quesadillas. Little did I know that you could make a vegan version that tastes just as good, if not better, and is healthy and nutritious. Ancho and chipotle are two types of Mexican chillies that give a real depth of flavour to the tempeh chorizo. Both ancho and chipotle are starting to become available in a few supermarkets, but I get my chilli spice blends from the www.thespicery.com, which makes amazing, fresh spice blends.

Serves 2

1 (200-gram) block tempeh, chopped into around 1-centimetre cubes
1 teaspoon ancho chilli powder or paste
2 teaspoons chipotle powder or paste (or to taste)
1 tablespoon soy sauce
1 tablespoon liquid smoke (optional)
2 tomatoes, diced
1 avocado, diced
1 red onion, finely diced
juice of 1/2–1 lime
salt
1 small pepper, finely chopped
2 teaspoons coconut oil, divided
1 tin chickpeas, drained and rinsed
1 tablespoon fajita spice
1/2 teaspoon garlic powder
30 grams cashew nut butter or soaked cashews
10 grams nutritional yeast
1/2 teaspoon garlic powder
80 grams thick unflavoured yoghurt (I like coconut)
2 tortillas (wholemeal, corn, or any other that you fancy)

1. Marinate chopped tempeh in chilli powders or pastes, soy sauce, and liquid smoke (if using). Leave to marinate for a few hours or overnight.

2. Just before you are ready to cook, make the salsa: combine tomatoes, avocado, onion, lime juice, and a big pinch of salt, adding more lime juice as needed.

3. Preheat the oven to 220°C. Line a baking sheet with foil.

4. Add tempeh and chopped pepper to prepared baking sheet. Cook 15–20 minutes; the tempeh should start to crisp up and char. Once cooked, set aside.

5. While tempeh is cooking, heat up a frying pan with 1 teaspoon coconut oil. Add chickpeas, fajita spice, garlic powder, and a big pinch of salt. Cook until hot.

6. Mash chickpeas with a fork or potato masher, or give the mixture a quick blitz in a blender. You want it to be a little rough, not smooth.

7. In a blender, combine cashew nut butter with nutritional yeast, garlic powder, and yoghurt. Blitz, adding a little water if required. You want the consistency of a thick cream.

8. In a large frying pan, heat the remaining 1 teaspoon coconut oil over medium-high heat.

9. Lay out your tortillas on a plate or board. Add half the chickpea mixture and spread out on one half of one tortilla (you will be folding it over), leaving a 1-centimetre space around the edge of the tortilla. Add half the cashew mixture, dotting it around and spreading it a little. Finally, add half the tempeh. Fold the opposite side of the tortilla over and repeat with the other tortilla.

10. Add the quesadillas to the pan (you may need to do one at a time depending on the size of your pan) and cook for a few minutes until the tortillas are starting to brown, then turn over.

11. When cooked, cut the quesadillas in half or thirds and plate up with the salsa. Enjoy on its own or with some chilli sauce (I like chipotle).

Chickpea and Sweet Potato Hash Enchilada

Enchiladas are like a Mexican version of lasagne. Don't be put off by the long list of ingredients. This comes together really easily, with little preparation required. It's healthy comfort food that is good for all seasons. I have used sweet potato here, but you can swap it for squash if you want to reduce the amount of carbohydrates or calories.

Serves 4

3 medium sweet potatoes, diced (no need to peel), or 250 grams squash (peeled)
120 grams cashews
1 spring onion, roughly chopped
1 tablespoon olive oil
1 red onion
2 tablespoons cumin seeds
2 peppers
3 cloves garlic, finely grated
2 tomatoes, roughly chopped
2 tins chickpeas, drained
4 teaspoons fajita spice mix

1 teaspoon chipotle paste or chilli flakes
couple handfuls of spinach
150 grams frozen peas
150 grams frozen sweetcorn
1/2 lime (optional)
corn or wholemeal wraps (depending on size, you might use 4–8)
2 tablespoons nutritional yeast
big pinch of salt
small bunch coriander, roughly chopped
chilli sauce, for serving

1. Place diced sweet potatoes in a large microwaveable bowl. Cover and cook on high power for 8 minutes. Meanwhile, boil water for soaking cashews.
2. Soak cashews and spring onion in 160 millilitres of just-boiled water.
3. In a large frying pan or saucepan over medium high heat, combine olive oil, red onion, cumin seeds, and peppers. Cook for a couple of minutes, then add garlic and tomatoes. Cook for another couple of minutes until onions are soft.
4. Add chickpeas, cooked sweet potatoes, fajita spice, and chipotle paste. Stir well, then mash up using a masher or large wooden spoon. You want it to be a rough mash (hash) so you have a mixture of textures.
5. Add spinach, peas, and sweetcorn. Cook until everything is warmed through. Add the juice of the lime (if using) and season to taste.
6. Preheat the oven to 200°C. Have a large baking dish (like a lasagne dish) ready.
7. Place roughly 2 heaped tablespoons of filling on a wrap. Roll it up so it is roughly the width of 2 fingers. Place in the baking dish and continue until the mixture is all used up. If you have used up all the wraps (or there is no more room for wraps) and still have mixture left, spread it over the top.
8. Place dish in the oven and bake for around 10 minutes, until wraps start crisping up.
9. Meanwhile, blend cashews, spring onion, their water, nutritional yeast, and salt. Pour over baked enchiladas, then sprinkle with coriander and serve with chilli sauce.

Chickpea Tikka Burgers

This has all the flavours of a naughty Indian takeaway, but with a whole lot of whole-food goodness. Although this may seem like a lot of ingredients, the recipe is easy to make, and putting it all together will take no more than 20–30 minutes. The oven then does the rest of the work.

You can make the burgers ahead of time and allow them to set in the fridge a little. If you don't have the time, though, they should still be fine.

Serves 2 (can easily double)

Burgers:
1 carrot, roughly chopped
4 spring onions
1 clove garlic, roughly chopped
1 centimetre ginger, roughly chopped
1 tin chickpeas, drained
1/2–1 chilli (depending on how spicy you like it), roughly chopped
small bunch coriander, roughly chopped
3 heaped teaspoons tikka paste
1 teaspoon garam masala
big pinch of salt, plus more to taste
60 grams of gram flour (chickpea flour)
1 teaspoon coconut oil, for cooking

Turmeric chips:
1 teaspoon coconut oil
2 medium floury potatoes (Maris Piper, King Edward, Desiree, etc.)
1 teaspoon turmeric
1/2 teaspoon garam masala
large pinch of salt
1 teaspoon arrowroot powder (found in baking sections of supermarkets; it helps crisp up the chips)
1 teaspoon mustard seeds
1 teaspoon sesame seeds

Cucumber raita:

1/3 cucumber
50 grams coconut yoghurt
a few mint leaves, finely chopped
salt

For serving:
Wholemeal pitta bread or vegan burger bun (optional)
sliced tomatoes
lettuce
mango chutney
chilli sauce

Make the burgers:

1. In a food processor, combine carrot, spring onions, garlic, and ginger. Blitz until everything is chopped.

2. Add the remaining burger ingredients to the food processor, except for gram flour and coconut oil. Blitz until combined. A few whole chickpeas will be fine. Taste for seasoning, then add the gram flour. Take out half the mixture in your hands and shape into a ball before flattening it into a burger (this can be done on a plate). Repeat with the other half and put in the fridge to firm up.

Make the chips:

3. Preheat oven to 200°C. Place a baking tray with 1 teaspoon coconut oil in the oven to heat up.

4. Cut potatoes (skin on) into 1-centimetre-wide chips. Place in a bowl with turmeric, garam masala, salt, and arrowroot. Coat thoroughly, then leave for a couple of minutes.

5. Place chips on preheated tray and coat with the melted coconut oil. Sprinkle with mustard seeds and sesame seeds and place in the oven for 30–35 minutes, mixing about halfway. When cooked, the chips should be crisp and golden.

6. **Cook burgers:**

7. After the chips have been in the oven for 15 minutes, heat up a frying pan on medium-high with 1 teaspoon coconut oil. When pan is hot, add burgers, cooking for around 5 minutes on both sides until starting to brown. Once cooked, transfer to a tray and cook in the oven for 5–10 minutes while you wait for the chips to be done.

Make cucumber raita:

8. While the burgers and chips are cooking, grate the cucumber. Squeeze all the water out. Mix grated cucumber with the coconut yoghurt and mint, adding a little salt. Set aside.

Serve:

9. When chips and burgers are about ready, toast pitta breads (if using). Cut open, then add raita, tomato slices, burger, lettuce, mango chutney, and chilli sauce. Serve with the chips.

South Indian Curry

Curries naturally lend themselves well to a plant-based diet. This curry is more South Indian inspired and uses curry leaves, which can be bought in some supermarkets. If you can't get your hands on any, don't let that put you off making it. It will taste delicious anyway. If you can get hold of fresh curry leaves, keep them in the freezer.

Serves 4

2 tablespoon coconut oil, divided

30 grams pistachios

30 grams cashews

1 small cauliflower, cut into bite-size florets

1 tablespoon cumin seeds

salt

1 onion, chopped

3 cloves garlic, finely grated

1 inch ginger, coarsely grated

1 tablespoon madras curry powder

8 curry leaves (optional)

1 tin coconut milk

2 tins chickpeas, drained and washed

200 grams frozen peas

2 handfuls mixed greens

2 teaspoons garam masala

wholegrain rice, for serving

mango chutney, for serving

1. Preheat oven to 220°C. Fill the kettle and bring to a boil. Place a baking tray with 1 tablespoon coconut oil in the oven as it heats.

2. Soak pistachios and cashews in boiling water.

3. Add cauliflower to heated baking tray with cumin seeds and a big pinch of salt. Mix thoroughly with melted oil. Roast for 20 minutes, or until cauliflower starts to brown.

4. In a large saucepan, heat remaining 1 tablespoon coconut oil over medium heat. Add onion, garlic, and ginger. Cook till onion just starts to colour (you may need to add a little water to stop the pan drying up).

5. Add curry powder and curry leaves. Cook for about 1 minute, so the spices are fragrant.

6. Add coconut milk, followed by chickpeas, adding a big pinch of salt and half a tin of water. Bring to a simmer, cover, and cook for 5 minutes

7. Drain the nuts. In a blender or food processor, combine nuts with around 100 millilitres water. You want to be able to blend the nuts to a smooth cream. Add a little more water if required. Once smooth, add the mixture to your curry.

8. Add peas, roasted cauliflower, mixed greens, and garam masala to the pan. Stir well and allow to simmer for a couple of minutes.

9. Serve with wholegrain rice and a good dollop of mango chutney.

Root Vegetable Dal

I love dal (or daal, or dhal)! The combination of spices and soothing lentils makes this a wonderful comfort food. Dal is amazingly nutritious and can be eaten on its own. My unusual twist is adding ginger and garlic after all the liquid has been added. This gives it a nice zing without being pungent. I have this for lunch most days, as one batch will last me most of the week. If having it after a workout, I would recommend you add extra carbs in the form of rice or naan.

Serves 6–8

600 grams red lentils, or 300 grams mung bean dal and 300 grams red lentils
1 tablespoon coconut oil
1 onion, roughly chopped
1 tablespoon cumin seeds
2 tablespoons madras curry powder
2 tablespoons garam masala
1 teaspoon chilli powder
1 teaspoon turmeric
salt
300 grams peas

4 carrots, peeled and chopped into 2-centimetre chunks
4 parsnips, peeled and chopped into 2-centimetre chunks
1 tablespoon soy sauce
1 tin chopped tomatoes
3 centimetres ginger, roughly chopped
4 cloves garlic, roughly chopped
2 handfuls kale, stemmed and roughly chopped

1. Wash the lentils, then soak in warm water while you prep the vegetables.

2. Fill the kettle and bring to a boil.

3. In a large saucepan, heat coconut oil over medium-high heat. Add onion and cumin seeds. When onion is starting to colour, add the rest of the spices, a big pinch of salt, and a little water to make a paste. Allow to cook for 30 seconds to 1 minute, adding more water if the pan starts to dry up.

4. Add peas, carrots, and parsnips, stirring and coating in the spice mix.

5. Drain and rinse lentils, then add to the pan, covering with water from the kettle. You want there to be about 2 inches of water above the lentils.

6. Add soy sauce and tinned tomatoes with their juices.

7. In a blender, combine ginger and garlic with 50 millilitres water (can add more if required) and blend till smooth. Add to the saucepan with plenty of salt.

8. Bring to a boil, then cover and simmer for 20—30 minutes or until lentils and vegetables are tender.

9. Add kale, stir, cover, and remove from heat. Allow kale to soften for 5 minutes before checking for seasoning and serving.

Sweet Potato and Chickpea Massaman

Massaman is a Thai curry that is mild, creamy, and warming. It is often made using beef and potatoes. I have replaced the beef with chickpeas and substituted sweet potatoes for the standard spud. If you want to reduce the number of calories, you could swap the sweet potato for butternut squash, which has half the amount.

Serves 4–6

1 tablespoon coconut oil
1 large red onion, sliced 1 centimetre thick
1 jar massaman curry paste (check if is veggie-friendly, as some pastes contain fish)
1 tin coconut milk
salt
2 medium sweet potatoes, cut into bite-size pieces
2 tins chickpeas, rinsed and drained
300 grams baby corn, cut in half, or sweetcorn
300 grams mange tout, cut in half or thirds, or peas
200 grams kale, stems removed, or spinach
80 grams crunchy whole-nut peanut butter
wholegrain rice (for serving)
fresh coriander, roughly chopped (for serving)

1. In a large saucepan, melt coconut oil over medium-high heat. Add sliced onion.

2. When onion is starting to colour, add massaman paste and fry for a couple of minutes, stirring regularly. Add coconut milk. Fill the tin up with water and add to the pan, then add another half a tin's worth of water with a couple of big pinches of salt.

3. Once liquid has come to a simmer, reduce heat to medium and add sweet potatoes and chickpeas. Cook for 8 minutes.

4. When sweet potatoes have just started to soften, add baby corn, mange tout, and kale. Cook until sweet potato is tender and vegetables still have a bit of texture.

5. Remove from heat and stir in peanut butter. Taste to season. Serve with wholegrain rice and chopped fresh coriander.

Teriyaki Tofu

A stir-fry is a great way to pack in plenty of vegetables, which you can change depending on the season. With a homemade teriyaki sauce, simple vegetables are elevated into something sweet, sticky, and comforting while remaining as healthy as possible. You can serve this on either wholegrain rice or noodles of your choice. (I am a sucker for udon noodles!)

Serves 2

1 tablespoon sesame oil
280 grams extra-firm tofu, cut into bite-size cubes
1 red onion, thickly sliced
2 cloves garlic, finely chopped
1 teaspoon finely chopped ginger
3–4 veg of your choice (such as broccoli, bok choi, carrot, pepper, cabbage, carrot, baby corn, green beans, or beansprouts), cut into thin batons
salt
4 spring onions, finely sliced

Teriyaki sauce:
1.5 tablespoons soy sauce
3 tablespoons maple syrup
1 tablespoon wine or cider vinegar
1 tablespoon water

1. In a large frying pan, heat sesame oil over a medium-high heat. Quickly add tofu and cook until starting to colour. Remove tofu from pan and set aside.

2. Keeping pan on heat, add onion, garlic, and ginger. Cook for about a minute, then start adding the veg, depending on how firm it is (for example, you would add carrot and broccoli first; wait for a few minutes before adding pepper, baby corn, or bok choi; and finally add beansprouts), and a big pinch of salt. Add small dashes of water as this helps the veg steam.

3. Combine all the sauce ingredients while the vegetables are cooking.

4. When all the veg is cooked to your liking, add tofu, spring onions, and sauce. Stir thoroughly, making sure everything is coated. Taste to season.

5. Serve with rice or noodles. You can add extra nutrition by adding some seaweed flakes and sesame seeds.

Kung Po Tofu

Sweet and spicy, this is a Chinese takeaway classic given the Jamie Beets vegan twist. Hopefully this will meet the need of your takeaway cravings. It should be quicker and healthier too!

Serves 2

3 tablespoons hoisin sauce

2 tablespoons red wine vinegar

1 tablespoon dark soy sauce (or regular if you can't get dark)

1/2 teaspoon dried chilli flakes (optional)

1 tablespoon coconut oil

280 grams extra-firm tofu, squeezed dry and crumbled

60 grams cashew nuts

1/2 teaspoon ground Sichuan peppercorns and 1/2 teaspoon salt, combined

200 grams tender-stem/purple sprouting or regular broccoli, florets cut off and stems cut in half lengthways if thick

130 grams baby corn, cut in half lengthways

salt

1 red pepper, cut into 1-centimetre slices

1 red onion, cut into 2-centimetre slices

glass of water, to have to hand

wholegrain rice

2 spring onions, sliced

1. In a small bowl, combine hoisin, vinegar, soy sauce, and chilli flakes.

2. In a wok or large frying pan, heat coconut oil over high heat. When it shimmers and starts to smoke, quickly add the tofu, cashews, and Sichuan pepper/salt mix. Stir and fry for 1–2 minutes.

3. Add broccoli and baby corn with a pinch of salt, stirring regularly for 2–3 minutes. Add a splash of water to create a little steam, allowing the veg to cook more quickly.

4. Throw in red pepper and red onion, a pinch of salt, and another splash of water if needed. Cook for about 2 minutes or until all the veg are nearly cooked.

5. Add hoisin mixture, stirring for around 30 seconds to make sure everything is coated. Check for seasoning, then serve over wholegrain rice with spring onion on top.

Tofu Laab (Cambodian Salad)

I first came across laab in Cambodia. It's a spicy, flavour-packed, refreshing salad, perfect for the summer. This version isn't authentic by any means, but it gets the flavours as close as possible, using easily available ingredients. You can marinate the tofu the day before to give it extra flavour and make preparing the meal even easier.

Serves 2

Sauce:

60 millilitres coconut water

40 millilitres lime juice

4 kaffir lime leaves, stems removed (if not available, you can use zest of 2 limes

2 sticks lemongrass, roughly sliced

2 pitted medjool dates (40 grams)

2-inch piece ginger, roughly sliced

2 tablespoons sriracha chilli sauce

4 teaspoons seaweed flakes

salt

Salad:

1 (225-gram) block extra-firm smoked tofu (nonsmoked can also be used)

2 shallots, sliced

handful green beans, blanched

1/3 cucumber, sliced into batons

For serving:

combined handful of mint, coriander, and Thai basil (optional), roughly chopped

2 tablespoons salted peanuts, roughly chopped

big twist of black pepper

wholegrain rice (optional)

Make the sauce:

In a food processor, combine all sauce ingredients and blitz. (This doesn't need to be a purée; it is OK to have small bits of lemongrass and ginger, as this will add texture and flavour to the dish.)

Make the salad:

Crumble tofu in a bowl and add 3/4 of the sauce. Stir and allow tofu to soak up the flavours. (This can be done up to a day in advance.)

In a large bowl, mix shallots, beans, and cucumber with remaining sauce. Add marinated tofu and give it a final mix, checking for seasoning.

Serve:

Serve laab in a wide bowl or plate. Garnish with fresh herbs, peanuts, and black pepper. Serve with wholegrain rice on the side, or serve laab on its own for a light meal.

Burger and Home Fries

This isn't the healthiest dish in the book, but it is healthier than a regular burger and fries, and having a treat now and then is a great way to live. Just try not to do it every day.

There are some really good vegan burgers out on the market. Some are even better than most beef burgers, and you could fool friends into thinking they are made of meat!

Home fries are an American potato dish that is generally unhealthy, but this version is oven-baked and much healthier, but just as tasty. You can use a combination of Maris Piper potatoes and sweet potatoes, or just one of them.

Serves 2

60 grams cashews
2 teaspoons coconut oil, divided
1 medium Maris Piper potato, chopped into 1- to 2-centimetre equal-sized pieces
1 medium sweet potato, chopped into 1- to 2-centimetre equal-sized pieces
1 red onion, finely sliced
1 large pepper, roughly chopped into 1–2-centimetre squares
1 tablespoon fajita spice
salt
1 teaspoon chipotle sauce (optional)
2 tablespoons nutritional yeast
1/2 teaspoon garlic powder
2 tablespoons ketchup
2 teaspoons mustard (French's the brand, not French mustard, is the best for this)
2 teaspoons liquid from the gherkins (see below)
2 vegan-friendly buns
2 plant-based burgers
slice of vegan cheese (optional)
1 large red onion, sliced into wedges
a few leaves iceberg lettuce, roughly chopped
1 large tomato, sliced
sliced gherkins

1. Bring kettle to a boil. Soak cashews in 80 millilitres boiled water.

2. Preheat oven to 220°C and place a roasting tin in the oven to warm up.

3. Add 1 teaspoon coconut oil to roasting tin and return to oven for 1 minute to melt. Take roasting tin out of the oven and add potatoes, onion, and pepper. Toss in the to cover

vegetables as evenly as possible. Add fajita spice and a large pinch of salt, and toss again. Place tin back in the oven for 20 minutes before you start with the burgers.

4. While home fries are cooking, in a blender or food processor, combine cashews with their soaking liquid, chipotle sauce, nutritional yeast, garlic powder, and a big pinch of salt. Set aside.

5. In a small mug, mix together the ketchup, mustard, and liquid from the gherkins. Set aside.

6. Heat up a frying pan over medium-high heat. (I like to toast the burger buns in the dry pan, or you could do it in the oven.) Add remaining 1 teaspoon coconut oil to the pan. Add burgers and cook to the packet instruction.

7. Two minutes before burgers are finished, add cheese and onion slices (unless you like your onion raw) and cover pan if possible. Allow steam to melt cheese and partially cook onion. Keep your eye on the home fries, making sure they don't overcook or get burnt.

8. Load up your buns with ketchup mixture, lettuce, tomato, gherkins, and cooked burgers.

9. Take home fries out of the oven and plate everything up. Pour cashew mixture over fries. Serve and enjoy.

Korean Burger with Sweet Potato Fries

Before I adopted a plant-based diet, I enjoyed a Korean-style burger and fries at a restaurant in London. The flavours were so strong and tasty, and I could still taste it long after I left the restaurant. One of the secrets to that flavour was a Korean chilli bean paste called *gochujang* that I was able to buy at my local Asian supermarket. I loved it and played around with it a lot in recipes. Now some supermarkets sell it, and people are starting to discover the amazing flavours of Korea.

This recipe is full of those flavours but only needs two Korean ingredients: gochujang and kimchi (Korean pickled cabbage). If you can't get hold of them, you can replace gochujang with your favourite chilli sauce and omit the kimchi. This recipe takes longer than other recipes in this book, so maybe do it when you have a bit more time available. A plant-based burger is a great, healthy weekend treat. To save a bit of time, buy firm tofu that doesn't require pressing (although we will still squeeze it a bit).

Serves 4

Burgers:
400 grams extra-firm tofu
400 grams mushrooms, roughly chopped
1 large bunch spring onions, roughly chopped
2-inch piece of ginger, grated
2 cloves garlic, grated
1 tablespoon sesame oil (plus a little more for the beansprouts)

1 tablespoon soy sauce
1 tablespoon gochujang sauce
1 tablespoon dark miso (optional)
salt
pepper
125 grams cooked quinoa, wholegrain rice, or a mixture of the two
30 grams ground flaxseed

Fries:
800 grams–1 kilogram sweet potato
1 tablespoon coconut oil
salt

1/2 teaspoon garlic powder

Gochujang mayo:
60 grams cashews nuts, soaked
50–60 millilitres water

1 tablespoon gochujang sauce
1/2 teaspoon white wine or cider vinegar

Finish:
1 tablespoon coconut oil
vegan-friendly burger buns
vegan-friendly kimchi (watch out for added fish!)

lettuce
cucumber
beansprouts

Make the burgers:

1. Wrap tofu in a kitchen towel and place under a bowl or plate with some tins on to squeeze out any water.
2. Heat a large pan over a medium heat.
3. In a food processor, combine mushrooms, spring onions, ginger, and garlic. Blitz until everything is chopped (don't over-process it).
4. Add sesame oil to heated pan, followed by mushroom mixture.
5. Add soy sauce, gochujang, and miso. Cook for about 12 minutes or until mixture has started to dry up. Add a good pinch of salt and pepper. Transfer to a large mixing bowl.
6. Put dry tofu in food processor and blitz until broken up, then add to mushroom mixture along with quinoa and ground flaxseed. Give it a good mix and taste for seasoning, adding more gochujang, salt, and pepper if required. If you want to eat more of it, you have nailed the seasoning!
7. Split the mixture into four equal balls and shape into burgers. Place on a plate and stick in the fridge for a couple of hours to firm up.

Make the fries:

8. Preheat oven to 220°C.
9. Peel sweet potatoes and cut into 1-centimetre slices lengthways. Now cut the slices into fries (about 1/2–1 centimetre thick).
10. Put 1 tablespoon coconut oil on a large baking tray and put it in the oven to warm up. Add sweet potato fries to the tray, coating in the oil and then the garlic powder and a big pinch of salt, ensuring there are evenly coated. Cook for around 30-40 minutes, when they should be starting to brown.

Make the gochujang mayo:

11. While fries are cooking, in a blender or food processor, blend together all the ingredients. Set aside.

Finish and serve:

12. In a large frying pan, heat 1 tablespoon coconut oil over medium heat. Add burgers and cook for 5 minutes on each side. Once you have turned the burgers, go back to your fries and turn them. Once the burgers are done in the pan, put them on a baking tray (or keep on the pan if it is ovenproof) and place in the oven for 5 minutes, by which time everything should be done.
13. Toast burger buns, then add mayo to both sides. Start layering up the fillings and your burger in the bun. Or, for a healthier option (and just as tasty), wrap the burger in some crisp lettuce.
14. Serve alongside fries and any extra mayo.

Jamie's Frying Pan Pizza Party!

Yes, pizza can be part of a healthy diet! I wasn't sure if I should include my pizza recipe in this book—not because I don't want to share it, but because it takes a lot of time. Pulling it together is fairly simple. The time-consuming part is letting the dough rest for twenty-four hours, as this is where the magic happens as the dough develops flavour. I use a mixture of wholemeal flour and spelt, but feel free to use just one of them.

The next part of making a great pizza is high heat! This can be challenging at home but there is a great hack that I use if I don't want to go outside and use my BBQ. It is a frying pan! You cook the base in the pan then add your toppings before sticking it under a hot grill.

You can buy vegan "cheese," but I prefer the taste of my cashew cheez sauce, and it has more nutritional benefit.

The recipe below is for the classic margherita, but you can choose whatever toppings you want. If you are looking for inspiration, you could try chickpeas, peppers, onions, chorizo tempeh, roasted aubergine, and one of my favourites, pistachio pesto, with roasted veg instead of tomato sauce (see recipe for Pesto Pasta).
Makes 4 pizzas that serves 4 (you can freeze these easily)

Dough:
250 grams strong wholemeal flour
250 grams spelt flour (or 500 grams of just one of the flours) plus extra for stretching
10 grams sugar (I like to use coconut sugar, you could use maple syrup too)
1 tablespoon olive oil

5 grams fresh yeast (available from some supermarkets or bakers) or 1/2 teaspoon dried yeast
300 grams cold water
1 tablespoon salt

Tomato sauce:
1 tin chopped tomatoes
1 garlic clove, finely chopped

1 tablespoon olive oil
1/2 teaspoon salt

Cashew cheez sauce:
120 grams cashews
4 tablespoons nutritional yeast

big pinch of salt

Garnish:
fresh basil
fresh tomato, sliced

olive oil

Make the dough:
1. The day before you plan on having the pizza, mix flours, sugar, olive oil, yeast, and water together, either using a mixer or by hand in a large bowl. Knead dough for 5 minutes, making sure all ingredients are combined. Cover with a kitchen towel and set aside for 30 minutes.

2. Once the 30 minutes are up, add salt and knead together with wet hands for around 3 minutes, after which the dough should be smooth and the salt well incorporated. Cover the bowl with cling film and place in the fridge for around 24 hours.

3. About 3–4 hours before eating, take dough out of the fridge. Place on a well-floured surface. You should have one big ball of dough. Press down on the dough a little and then bring one end of the dough to the middle, followed by the other end. Rotate 90 degrees and do the same, then flatten slightly.

4. Place bowl onto kitchen scales, then add dough. Divide by 4 and cut dough off to make equal sizes. You should now have 4 pieces of dough that are of equal weight.

5. Just like you did with the big dough, fold each piece of dough on itself, rotate 90 degrees, and repeat. Now tuck the edges of the dough underneath and push into the middle. Using well-floured hands, shape dough into a ball and put onto a well-floured large tray. Repeat with the remaining dough. Cover with a kitchen towel and set aside at room temperature for 3–4 hours. You want the dough to have doubled in size. The warmer the room, the quicker the process will be. If the kitchen is cold, find a warm space like an airing cupboard.

Make the sauces:

6. Fill the kettle and bring to a boil.

7. Make tomato sauce by combining all sauce ingredients and mixing by hand or with a fork.

8. Make cheez sauce by adding 140 grams just-boiled water to the cashews and soaking for 10 minutes or more. When you are ready to make the sauce, combine with the remaining ingredients in a blender and blitz until smooth.

Prepare the pizza:

9. Heat up the grill to its highest heat and place a dry non-stick frying pan on the highest heat.

10. Place dough balls on a well-floured surface and one ball at a time, press down with your palm, working from the centre and moving out. This first part helps create the round base. Now either push with your palms (to keep a puffy crust) or take a rolling pin and roll/stretch horizontally from the middle and away from you, then again from the middle and toward you. Turn the dough 90 degrees and repeat the process until you have a base the size of your frying pan.

11. Add a little olive oil to the pan (optional) and carefully lift the pizza dough on your knuckles, trying to keep its shape. Carefully place the dough in the frying pan and push the dough out to cover the base, being careful not to burn yourself. Add the tomato sauce and toppings onto the dough. After a couple of minutes carefully lift up the dough using a spatula and check the base. You are looking for a dark, golden crust. Once the crust is golden, place the pan underneath the grill, as high to the heat as possible. Cook until the crust is golden (2-4 minutes). Take the pan out from under the grill and plate up.

12. Garnish pizza with fresh basil, tomato slices, and a good drizzle of extra virgin olive oil. Slice, serve, and repeat the process with the remaining dough until all the dough has been used.

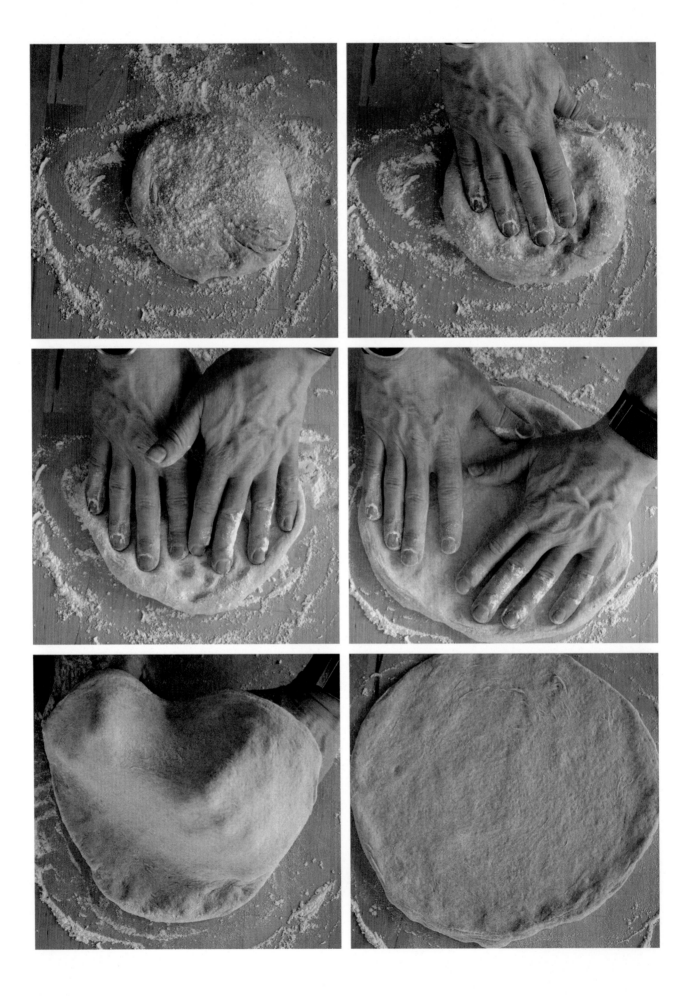

Pesto Pasta

There's nothing like the superfresh smell of basil. Moving to a plant-based diet doesn't mean you need to miss out on pesto. This version is really fresh and easy to make. You can use lentil, chickpea, or pea pasta to boost the protein content.

Serves 2

30 grams pistachios
30 grams almonds or pine nuts, or a mixture of the two
150–250 grams pasta (wholemeal, lentil, chickpea, or pea)
salt
160 grams peas
bunch of basil, about 25 grams
2 tablespoons nutritional yeast
juice of 1 lemon
2 tablespoons olive oil
pepper
2 big handfuls spinach
4 sun-dried tomatoes or 1 large tomato, roughly chopped

1. Fill the kettle and bring to a boil. Soak nuts in freshly boiled water and set aside.

2. Cook pasta in remaining water, adding 10–15 grams salt.

3. When pasta has about 3 minutes left, add peas.

4. To make the pesto, drain nuts and add to blender with 100 millilitres water, basil (save a few leaves for garnish), nutritional yeast, lemon juice, olive oil, and a big pinch of salt and pepper. Blitz until smooth and taste to season, adding more lemon juice if required. Set aside.

5. Drain cooked pasta and peas and return to pan. Add pesto, spinach, and sun-dried tomatoes. Taste to season. Serve with remaining basil leaves

Tofu "Paneer" Sag Aloo Tray Bake

A tray bake is an easy way to feed a few people. This is a pretty simple tray bake that can be prepped and done partly ahead of time, so all you need to do is stick it in the oven. The marinating of the tofu in the spices and nutritional yeast gives it a great flavour and cheesy taste that is reminiscent of paneer. I have included two different yoghurt dressings to go with it—one by me and one by a friend, Lizzie Mango, who made it off the cuff when I was making this dish for a few friends.

Serves 4

100 grams coconut yoghurt
40 grams nutritional yeast
2 teaspoons ground turmeric, divided
2 teaspoons curry powder, divided
2 teaspoons garam masala, divided
splash plant-based milk
2 (280-gram) blocks extra-firm tofu, cut into 1-centimetre cubes
salt
800 grams Maris Piper potatoes, skin left on, chopped into large wedges
mixture of seasonal vegetables (such as cauliflower, broccoli, carrots, peas)
2 teaspoons coconut oil
2 teaspoons cumin seeds
1 teaspoon mustard seed (optional)
1/2 teaspoon chilli powder, or more if you like it spicy
2 white onions, cut into 1-centimetre wedges
200 grams baby leaf spinach
mango chutney, for serving

My dressing:
150 grams coconut yoghurt
1/2 cucumber, cored and grated
juice of 1/2 lemon
8–10 mint leaves, finely chopped

Lizzie's dressing
150 grams coconut yoghurt
2 spring onions, finely chopped
juice of 1/2 lime
1 tablespoon tahini
splash plant-based milk

1. In a large bowl, mix together coconut yoghurt, nutritional yeast, 1 teaspoon of the turmeric, 1/2 teaspoon of the curry powder, and 1 teaspoon of the garam masala. You may need to add a splash of milk to loosen it up. Add tofu to the mixture along with 2 big pinches of salt. Set aside to marinate. This can be anywhere between 30 minutes and overnight.

2. Preheat oven to 220°C.

3. In a large pot, cook potato wedges in well-salted boiling water for 5–8 minutes. You want to just about be able to stick a fork in them. Drain, saving the water, and set the potatoes aside until you want to cook everything else.

4. Cut the veg into suitable size for roasting—for example, broccoli and cauliflower into large florets and carrots into thin wedges. The denser the veg, the finer you will have to chop it.

5. Bring reserved water from potatoes back to a boil and add cauliflower (you can also add the broccoli if you wish). Cook for about 5 minutes, just to soften it up. Drain and set aside.

6. Pour coconut oil on a large baking tray and place in the oven. Once hot, add potatoes, cumin, mustard seed (if using), a big pinch of salt, and remaining turmeric, curry powder, and garam masala. Place tray in the oven and cook for 15 minutes.

7. While everything is in the oven, make either of the dressings by mixing all the ingredients together. You may need to add a splash of plant-based milk to loosen it up, as you want to be able to drizzle it over the curry.

8. After 15 minutes, remove tray from the oven and add chopped veg and onion, leaving any small veg, such as peas, until the end. Add another big pinch of salt and mix well.

9. Now add the tofu and all its marinade. Mix carefully so you don't break up the tofu. Stick the tray back in the oven and cook until potatoes are golden and crisp.

10. Add spinach and any small vegetables with another pinch of salt. Place back in the oven to wilt the spinach for a couple of minutes.

11. Serve with the dressing of your choice and some mango chutney on the side.

Chilli sin Carne

This sweet and smoky dish takes a bit of time to prepare but is well worth it and will give you enough chilli for up to six people. If you can't get hold of chipotle paste (chipotle is smoked jalapeño), you could use chilli powder or fresh chillies. If you are looking to increase the protein content, you could add some tempeh chorizo (see recipe for Quesadillas). You can eat this either with quinoa, rice, or sweet potato to serve more people, or have it on its own with avocado or guacamole, which will give you about four servings.

Serves 4–6

1 tablespoon olive oil
1 onion, chopped
3 cloves garlic, roughly chopped
1 tablespoon cumin seeds
3 tablespoons maple syrup
1 tablespoon fajita spice
2 teaspoons chipotle paste
1/2 teaspoon cinnamon
6 portobello mushrooms, finely sliced
125 dried red lentils, rinsed
2 tins beans, drained (your choice of black beans, pinto, kidney, borlotti, chickpeas, etc. (I like a mix)

2 cooked beetroot, roughly diced
500 millilitres passata
2 vegetable stock cubes
120 grams cashews
2 spring onions, roughly chopped
4 tablespoons nutritional yeast
salt
couple of handfuls of spinach
sweet potato, baked in the oven/ microwaved, or quinoa
avocado or guacamole

1. In a large saucepan, heat olive oil over medium heat. Add onion, garlic, and cumin seeds. When onion starts to colour, add maple syrup, fajita spice, chipotle paste, and cinnamon. Stir and cook for 30 seconds.

2. Add mushrooms and cook until starting to brown.

3. Add lentils, beans, beetroot, passata, 500 millilitres water, and stock cubes. Bring to a simmer before covering pan and allowing the chilli to simmer until lentils are soft, about 30 minutes.

4. While chilli is cooking, soak cashews in 180 grams freshly boiled water. Add spring onions, nutritional yeast, and a big pinch of salt. Set aside.

5. Once cooked, stir in spinach, remove from heat, taste, and season. Blitz the cashew mixture together in a blender or food processor to make a smooth paste.

6. Serve chilli with a sweet potato or quinoa, the cashew cream sauce, and guacamole or avocado.

Spicy Peanut Noodles

This is a simple meal which can be made with a mixture of vegetables, so don't feel you have to use exactly what I've used. I roast the vegetables, as I find it easier than using a pan or wok. Feel free to do what works best for you. Roasted broccoli in the oven always tastes great though. If you are looking for extra protein, then use soba noodles, which are made from buckwheat, as they are high in protein.

Serves 1 (easy to double)

100 grams tenderstem or sprouting broccoli, halved
1/2 red onion, cut into 1-centimetre slices
1 pepper, cut into 1-centimetre slices
1 clove garlic, grated
2 centimetres ginger, grated
2 tablespoons soy sauce, divided
40 grams crunchy peanut butter
1 tablespoon balsamic vinegar
1 teaspoon or more chilli sauce (I like Korean gochujang)
90 grams vegan-friendly noodles (I like soba or udon)
sesame seeds (optional)

1. Preheat oven to 190°C.

2. Add broccoli, onion, and pepper to a baking tray. Stick in oven for 10 minutes.

3. In a small bowl, combine garlic, ginger, and 1 tablespoon of the soy sauce.

4. When veg has been in the oven for 10 minutes, add soy sauce mixture and roast for another 5–10 minutes, until the broccoli starts to colour.

5. In a medium bowl, mix together peanut butter, remaining 1 tablespoon soy sauce, vinegar, and chili sauce.

6. Cook noodles to package instructions.

7. When everything has cooked, mix noodles, veg, and sauce together in the pan you cooked the noodles in and serve. Top with sesame seeds

Tempeh BLAT (Bacon, Lettuce, Avocado, and Tomato)

One of the reasons many people say they can't go vegan is they would miss bacon too much. There are now plant-based versions of bacon available in shops, but if you want that smoky and salty taste in a less processed and healthier way, then a tempeh BLAT is for you. I have added avocado into the classic BLT mix, as it adds a satisfying fatty mouthfeel to contrast with the "meaty" tempeh. If you want to reduce the calories, feel free to serve it on one piece of bread that has been toasted. It tastes just as good! If you can't get hold of liquid smoke, you could use smoked paprika, chipotle powder or sauce, or just omit it. If you *can* get liquid smoke, it is worth having in the cupboard, as you may be making this a lot!

Serves 2

1 (200-gram) block tempeh, sliced 5 millimetres thick lengthways
1 tablespoon liquid smoke (can be found in the sauce section of some supermarkets)
1/2 tablespoon maple syrup
2 tablespoons soy sauce
1 teaspoon chipotle sauce (optional)
2 teaspoons coconut oil
vegan mayo
chipotle sauce (optional)
4 slices of bread
2 tomatoes, sliced
1 avocado, cut in half, pitted, and sliced
a few leaves crispy lettuce
salt

1. Marinate the tempeh in a mixture of liquid smoke, maple syrup, soy sauce, and chipotle sauce. Leave at least a couple of hours or overnight.

2. In a large frying pan, heat coconut oil over medium-high heat. Add marinated tempeh. Fry on each side until starting to brown and crisp up.

3. While tempeh is cooking, spread vegan mayo and chipotle sauce (if using), on the bread slices.

4. Start layering all the ingredients, including the cooked tempeh, on the bread, adding a pinch of salt to the tomatoes and avocado slices.

5. Slice in half and enjoy warm.

Stuffed Sweet Potato

Who doesn't love a stuffed potato? This version combines comfort food and healthy nutrition all in one easy meal.

Serves 2

60 grams cashews

2 sweet potatoes (about 250 grams each), washed and halved lengthwise

1 tin black beans, drained

160 grams corn

2 spring onions, finely sliced, plus 1 (optional) for cashew sauce

2 teaspoons fajita or Cajun spice

2 teaspoons dried oregano

2 teaspoons ground cumin

1 1/2 teaspoons dried garlic

1 avocado, peeled, pitted, and chopped

1 large tomato, chopped

1/2 red onion, finely chopped

small bunch of coriander, finely sliced

small clove garlic, finely grated

juice of 1/2–1 lime

1 spring onion (optional)

2 tablespoons nutritional yeast

salt

1. In a kettle, boil a small amount of water. Place cashews in a mug and pour over 80 millilitres freshly boiled water. Set aside until the end.

2. Microwave sweet potatoes on full power for 6–8 minutes, until cooked through (this can be done ahead of time, even a couple of days before). Allow to cool, then scoop out the flesh, taking care not to damage the skins, and place in a large mixing bowl.

3. Preheat oven to 210°C.

4. To the bowl with the sweet potato flesh, add black beans, corn, 2 spring onions, fajita spice, oregano, cumin, and garlic. Mix thoroughly and taste to season.

5. Place potato skins in the oven for 15–20 minutes, when they should be starting to crisp up.

6. When potato skins are crisp, quickly heat up the sweet potato mixture in the microwave. Fill potato skins with sweet potato mixture. Bake 10–15 minutes.

7. While stuffed sweet potatoes are baking, mash avocado to a rough paste, then add tomato, onion, coriander, garlic, and lime juice. Taste guacamole to season, adding more lime juice and salt if required.

8. In a blender, combine cashews and their soaking liquid with spring onion (if using), nutritional yeast, and a good pinch of salt. Blitz until smooth, adding water if required. Taste to season.

9. When everything is ready, plate up the stuffed sweet potatoes, drizzle the cashew sauce over, and serve with guacamole on the side.

Hummus on Sourdough with Chopped Salad

Hummus is so easy to make, and this humble dish is elevated by the fresh chopped salad, which gives it a sharpness, freshness, and texture.

Serves 1 (easy to double)

Salad:
1 medium tomato, roughly chopped
1/2 small red onion, finely chopped
1/2 avocado, peeled, pitted, and roughly chopped
1/4 cucumber, halved, cored, and roughly chopped
juice of 1/2 lemon
1 teaspoon olive oil
salt and pepper

For serving:
1 slice sourdough bread
1 portion hummus (see recipe at the end of this chapter)
salt and pepper

1. In a large bowl, mix together all the salad ingredients. Taste to season.

2. Toast your sourdough under the grill. Once done, spoon a thick layer of hummus on, followed by the salad. Finish with a pinch of salt and pepper. Serve fresh.

Quinoa

Quinoa is really versatile and has a lot of health and nutritional benefits, including B vitamins, iron, potassium, calcium, and vitamin E. It's also a great source of protein, fibre, manganese, zinc, and magnesium. However, it can be really difficult to cook. I have discovered a foolproof way to make it—as long as you have a microwave.

I like to make a large batch of quinoa to keep in the fridge for up to a week (you could also freeze it). It can be used as a grain to go with a main dish; as a base for a salad; or even as a porridge.

1. In a large microwaveable bowl, combine 1 cup quinoa with 2 cups of water and a pinch of salt.
2. Cover and cook on full power for 7 minutes.
3. Uncover, stir, and cook for another 4 minutes.
4. Let stand for a few minutes before stirring.

Quinoa Salad

If you plan on having this salad a few times during the week, you can make a few portions of the dressing and keep in the fridge.

Serves 1

Dressing:
Makes 1 portion
1 teaspoon olive oil
1 teaspoon acid (lime or vinegar, such as balsamic, cider, or sherry)

1 teaspoon tahini (sesame seed butter)
splash soy sauce
pinch salt and pepper
chilli sauce (if you like it spicy)

For the salad:
150–180 grams cooked quinoa
half a tin of beans/lentils (I like to use black beans or green lentils)
Choose 3 or 4 of the following:
peas
sweetcorn

avocado
spinach
pepper
spring onion
pineapple
tomatoes

1. In a dressing pot or jar, combine dressing ingredients and shake till it comes together.

2. In a large bowl, combine salad ingredients with dressing and mix well.

Gazpacho Soup

This recipe came about after my body was craving some veg, and I wanted a quick snack. This will also make a nice meal on a hot day. Just serve with some good-quality bread.

Serves 2 as a snack or 1 as a main (with bread)

1 tin chopped tomatoes
1 tin butter beans, rinsed and drained
3 spring onions, roughly chopped
2 handfuls spinach (optional, as it will make the soup much darker)
1 red pepper, roughly chopped
1/2 cucumber, roughly chopped
2 tablespoons red wine vinegar
1 tablespoon smoked paprika
pinch of garlic powder
good pinch of salt
twist of pepper
olive oil, to finish
a few mint leaves, finely sliced

1. In a blender, combine all but the last two ingredients. Blend until smooth; taste to season.

2. Serve in a bowl with a drizzle of olive oil and the mint.

Coleslaw

If you have a food processor with a grater and slicer attachment, making a quick coleslaw couldn't be easier. It's a great way to get in some extra vegetables and their nutrients. You can adapt it to make it seasonal. I try to aim for at least three different vegetables and rarely use mayonnaise. Using acid (vinegar or citrus juice) and salt is often good enough. Below are just suggestions, so feel free to make your own combinations up. If you don't have a food processor, you can do this by hand with a good knife and a box grater for the carrots.

Serves 4

1/3 head white or red cabbage, cut into pieces that will fit in your food processor
1/2 red onion or 1 or 2 spring onions
4 small carrots, washed
juice of 1/2–1 lime or lemon or 1 tablespoon vinegar
salt

1. Add cabbage pieces to food processor. Use the thick slicing blade attachment, push the cabbage down with a guard until completely sliced.

2. Push red onion through on the same setting or slice by hand. (If using spring onions, finely slice by hand.) Transfer cabbage and onion to a large bowl.

3. Put the coarse grater attachment into the food processor and grate carrots, adding to bowl with onion and cabbage.

4. Add lime juice and a big pinch of salt; toss thoroughly. Taste to test the seasoning, adding more acid and salt if required. If you keep wanting to eat it, you have nailed the seasoning!

5. Set aside for 5 minutes and taste again, adjusting seasoning as required.

Tip: Other ingredients that could be added include pomegranate seeds, fennel, radish, apples, celery, peppers, cucumber, herbs, mustard, mayonnaise, and yoghurt.

Hummus

Hummus is so easy to make and can be made from store cupboard essentials. Making it at home is healthier and cheaper than buying a store-bought version. Feel free to add different ingredients to mix it up, such as sun-dried tomatoes or roasted peppers. Try to get the mixture as smooth as possible by adding a little extra water as you go. The more water you add, the more you will need to season it. Traditionally, water isn't used, just oil and lemon juice, but water helps create a smooth texture without adding extra calories from oil.

Serves 1–2

1 tin chickpeas, drained
1 small clove garlic
2 teaspoons tahini (sesame seed paste, available in most supermarkets)
1–2 tablespoons olive oil
juice of 1/2 lemon
big pinch of salt

1. In a blender or food processor, combine all ingredients along with a splash of water and blitz till smooth, adding more water if required.

2. Taste to season, adding more lemon juice or salt if required.

3. Serve with wholemeal pita bread or batons of carrot, cucumber, or celery.

Desserts and Sweet Snacks

I admit it! I have a sweet tooth! However, sweet doesn't have to mean unhealthy. Here are a few dishes that will hopefully satisfy your sweet tooth too.

Apple and Blackberry Crumble

Moving to a plant-based diet doesn't mean you have to miss out on a good old crumble. Far from it! This plant-based take makes it healthy with all the warming autumnal comfort of any other. I have swapped the traditional cream/custard for vanilla-flavoured soya yoghurt.

Serves 4

2 bananas
3 pitted medjool dates
juice of half a lemon
3 large cooking apples, peeled, cored, and chopped into 1-centimetre chunks
500g grams blackberries or mixed berries (can use frozen)
1 tablespoon coconut oil
100 grams oats
1 tablespoon maple syrup
1 teaspoon vanilla extract
vanilla-flavoured plant-based yoghurt, for serving

1. In a food processor or blender, combine bananas, dates, lemon juice, and a little water. Blend until smooth.

2. Preheat oven to 175°C.

3. In a medium sized baking dish, add the apple, banana mixture, and berries.

4. In a large bowl rub the coconut oil with the oats, maple syrup and and vanilla; give it a stir. Sprinkle over apple and blackberry mixture, then bake until oats start to go golden, around 45 -50 minutes.

5. Serve with a good dollop of plant-based vanilla yoghurt.

Rawesome Ultra Marathon Bars

A peanut chocolate caramel bar. Sound familiar? But this one is healthy, with oats, seeds and nuts in it. To avoid any copyright confusion, and because each bar weighs over 75 grams, I give you rawesome ultra marathon bars! Since they're raw, there is no need to turn the oven on. All you need is a food processor. Feel free to halve the mix, but you'll wish you'd made a full batch. Soaking the dates in hot water will help the mixture bind together a bit easier.

Makes 8–16 bars

Bars:
100 grams oats
50 grams sunflower seeds
280 grams pitted medjool dates
100 grams smooth peanut butter
6 teaspoons cacao
2 teaspoons maca powder
pinch of salt

Coating:
100 grams crunchy peanut butter
20 grams maple syrup
2 teaspoons cacao
1 teaspoon maca powder
pinch of salt

1. In a food processor, combine oats and sunflower seeds. Blitz to make a fine flour.

2. Add the rest of the bar ingredients and blitz until combined.

3. Using your hands, take the mixture out of the food processor and make sure everything has come together. Keep working it until there is not a crumb left. If you find it is struggling to come together, add a splash or water.

4. Shape into individual bars (around 75 grams each, if going for the full size) or smaller cubes or balls. Put in a box or on a plate.

5. Mix coating ingredients together and spoon about a teaspoon onto each bar until all the coating has been used up.

6. Store in the fridge for a couple of hours before eating—if you can wait that long! It lasts well for a week, or you can freeze.

Blueberry Muffins

Having an easy, healthy snack is a great way to keep the temptation of other food away. These muffins are perfect for that and will keep nicely in the fridge for five days. Just take however many you plan to eat out of the fridge to let come to room temperature, or quickly heat them up in the microwave. I don't bother putting the mixture in muffin cases. If you have a good greaseproof or silicone tray, the mixture can go straight in and will come out well. You can have one or two as a snack or two to three as a breakfast.

Makes 12 muffins

240 grams oats
25 grams ground flaxseed
1 tablespoon cinnamon
1 teaspoon bicarbonate of soda
3 ripe bananas, roughly 280 grams (the riper the better)
5 pitted medjool dates, about 80 grams
120 millilitres plant-based milk
juice of half a lemon
200 grams blueberries (frozen is fine)
pinch of salt

1. Preheat oven to 170°C.

2. In a food processer, blitz the oats, then place in a large mixing bowl with the ground flaxseed, cinnamon, and bicarbonate of soda.

3. In the food processor, blitz together bananas, dates, milk, and lemon juice. When smooth, add to the oat mixture. Add blueberries and salt and stir well.

4. Add large spoonfuls of the mixture to a greaseproof muffin tin, evenly sharing it out. Place in oven and cook 20–25 minutes, until muffins start to go golden.

5. Cool on a rack before storing in the fridge.

Mango Lassi

On a hot day, nothing beats a mango lassi to refresh you and get some vitamins in. Originating as a yoghurt-based drink from India, this plant-based version is just as good as any you will find, and it's good for you. Enjoy this as a snack or dessert, or add some oats (40–60 grams) for a breakfast smoothie. I have added a little turmeric and black pepper (when paired together, their power is enhanced), which have anti-inflammatory, antioxidant, and disease-fighting qualities.

Serves 1

80 grams frozen mango
80 grams frozen pineapple
1/2–1 banana
200 grams plant-based milk
100 grams plant-based vanilla or coconut yoghurt
pinch of turmeric and ground black pepper (optional)
juice of half a lime (optional)

Place everything in a blender and blitz until smooth. Put on your sunglasses and enjoy! Summer in a glass!

Mango and Pineapple Nice Cream

What's *nice cream*? Nice cream is where you blitz frozen fruit together with frozen banana and as little liquid as possible (depending on the power of your blender or food processor) to create a smooth ice-cream-like consistency. If you don't feel your blender is strong enough, you could let the frozen fruit sit at room temperature for 5 minutes.

I keep frozen bananas in a freezer bag in the fridge and add to them as needed. Make sure you cut the banana into bite-size pieces to help your food processor. The frozen banana really helps create a smooth texture and binds it all together. Feel free to play around with other fruit combinations.

Serves 2

160 millilitres plant-based milk
160 grams frozen pineapple
160 grams frozen mango
100–200 grams frozen banana
pinch of turmeric
pinch of pepper
scoop vanilla or banana protein (optional)
granola (optional)
almond butter (optional)

1. In a food processor or powerful blender, combine milk (you may need extra) and frozen fruit. You can wait 5 minutes to let the fruit soften slightly or blitz straight away. Blitz until smooth, adding more milk if needed.

2. Add turmeric, pepper, and protein powder (if using). Blitz again.

3. Scoop into bowls and top with granola or almond butter.

My Chocolate Valentine Smoothie

I threw this together just trying to get in some fruit I hadn't had that day. I was surprised how good it was! It tasted like a really nice version of a strawberry chocolate. It's also a great way of squeezing in some superhealthy spirulina.

Serves 1

70 grams frozen blueberries
70 grams frozen strawberries
1 medium-sized banana
200 millilitres water
1 teaspoon cacao
1/2 scoop chocolate flavour plant-based protein (optional)
1/2 teaspoon spirulina (optional)

In a blender, combine all ingredients and blitz till smooth. Serve in a glass.

Blueberry and Peanut Butter Chia Pot

This is the easiest, simplest recipe in the book, and one of the tastiest! The chia seeds help set the yoghurt so it has a mousse-like consistency. You could have this as a snack or impress guests and serve it in a nice glass as dessert.

Serves 1

130 grams plant-based yoghurt (I like to use vanilla soy yoghurt)
50 grams blueberries
20 grams chia
1 teaspoon peanut butter
granola, to finish

1. In a pot or glass, combine everything except the granola and stir till combined. Refrigerate for a minimum of 20 minutes or overnight.

2. Serve with a small sprinkling of granola.